# COMPASS POINTS

Lynne Hackles' Handy Hints is a collection of tips and advice she has gathered over her years of selling words. Written in bite-sized pieces, all are useful, some are funny, and all are positive. Another excellent book from one of our most talented and amusing writing tutors.
**Suzanne Ruthven**, Editor - The New Writer

Only Lynne Hackles could write a book of Handy Hints for Writers. She's been giving advice to writers for many years (despite being only 21!) and has collected thousands of tips from the numerous authors and writers she's interviewed for her regular column in *Writing magazine*. I particularly love the hint about creating a Great Aunt that you can offer as an excuse when a non-writer asks you to do something you don't want to do. This is one of those books you read from cover to cover and then dip back into, from time to time. Very handy indeed!
**Simon Whaley**, author of *The Positively Productive Writer*

Witty and wonderful, insightful and inspiring. If you write, want to write or know anybody who thinks there's a book lurking inside them, buy this guide...
Every writer needs a friend like Lynne Hackles. This book is the next best thing.
I love Lynne's humour and her quirky way of looking at life's truths. Essential reading for all scribes.
**Jane Wenham-Jones**, *Wannabe a Writer* and *Wannabe A Writer We've Heard Of*

If you only buy one How To Write book, make it this one. Lynne Hackles has a wealth of experience, and tells you everything you need to know with wit, wisdom, insight and humour. Nor has she forgotten how scary it is to be starting out on the long, winding, rocky road to publication. Lynne is a guide you can trust. She will tell you what, and show you how. The rest is up to you.

**Jane Jackson**, *A Place of Birds; The Iron Road; Dangerous Waters; Tide of Fortune; Eye of the Wind; The Chain Garden.*

# Compass Points

## Handy Hints for Writers

# Compass Points

## Handy Hints for Writers

## Lynne Hackles

**COMPASS**
**BOOKS**

Winchester, UK
Washington, USA

First published by Compass Books, 2013
Compass Books is an imprint of John Hunt Publishing Ltd., Laurel House, Station Approach,
Alresford, Hants, SO24 9JH, UK
office1@jhpbooks.net
www.johnhuntpublishing.com
www.compass-books.net

For distributor details and how to order please visit the 'Ordering' section on our website.

Text copyright: Lynne Hackles 2012

ISBN: 978 1 84694 845 9

A CIP catalogue record for this book is available from the British Library.

Design: Lee Nash

Printed and bound in the USA by Edwards Brothers Malloy

We operate a distinctive and ethical publishing philosophy in all
areas of our business, from our global network of authors to
production and worldwide distribution.

# CONTENTS

# 1

# In the beginning

### Need an intro? Here's mine.

'I wish I knew then what I know now.' Have you ever said that? If so I'm here to help.

I'm going to pass on what I've learned over thirty years of writing.

Some of these tips and snippets of advice may not work for you. Or they may work but only some of the time. Many contradict each other because that's the way writing goes – there are no hard and fast rules in writing. What works for one person will do nothing for another. What works one day may not work the next.

Every time we sit down to write the process may be different.

If there is one Golden Rule it is not to beat yourself up about your work.

A lifetime ago I read an article on how to write a best-seller. The author of this piece gave advice which included always using green ink, standing on your head in the shower to write and to be sure to commit suicide a week before their book came out. (Not advised here.)

Now, fancy me remembering that! It could be proof that my daftest tips will stick with you. Forever. It may be that the silliest will work for you. Often. All I can say is that they've all worked for me, even if it was only the once.

### Coming out

At some point you will want or feel the need to tell others what you are doing. 'I want to be a writer.' Or 'I am a writer.'

One of my all-time favourite quotes comes from Molière who said,

'Writing is like prostitution.
First you do it for the love of it,
Then you do it for a few friends
And finally you do it for money.'

Some people write in secret simply because they love the act of writing and they want to put their thoughts and ideas down on paper or up on screen. That's doing it for love but how long can you spend locked away on your own before a family member wants to know what you are up to? At some point, unless you live alone and can keep Big Secrets, you will want to come out and admit that you are writing. This is when you begin sharing your work with a few friends and we all know friends will tell you how good you are and how you should get published. This is the stage when you might join other writers at a club or group or class and, when you are good enough, they might encourage you to write for money.

So the stages of writing are:

1. for Love
2. for Friends
3. for Money

We all need to hold on to stage one. Lots are happy with stage two. Many dream of stage three. Some reach it and end up happy, earning money by doing something they love.

There's nothing wrong with any of the above as long as you are happy being at whatever stage you've reached.

## The best advice ever
Find the market first. Write the product next.

## Write about what you know
It's what all new writers are told and it does make life easier. If

you know a subject then you don't need to do any/as much research.

Work out what you actually do know. Try making a list. Add hobbies, interests, jobs ... in fact you know such a lot because it's all down to personal experience and the longer you've lived the more personal experience you've had.

I bet you don't realise how wise and clever you are.

## Write about what you don't know

Learn by exploring unfamiliar areas. Check out the non-fiction section of the local library. Take up a new sport or hobby. Learn and write about it. Use your imagination and invent a whole new world.

Try to learn something new every day. Visit a new place. Make a new friend. Try out a new word. Have a new experience. (Make it a legal one.)

## Not in your head

Many people write books in their heads. Make sure yours is written on screen or paper.

## Kissing babies

I always did it discreetly. Kissing.

Standing near the post box I would take a good look around to make sure no-one was watching. Non-writers wouldn't understand if they saw me plant my lips on the large envelope before dropping it into the post box. They'd think I was mad. Kissing lottery tickets is okay but members of the non-writing community don't understand about manuscripts.

I often wondered if any eagle-eyed receptionist, whose job it was to open the post in the mornings, wondered what the Peach Crush smudge on the envelope was. It's not a good way to blot one's lippie. But my babies were always kissed before being sent out into that big wide world. Why? Because that's what I did with the very first piece I submitted and it was accepted so it stands to reason, doesn't it, that every one after that needed to be kissed to stand any chance of success.

Now, when most work is delivered via email, I still pucker up before pressing SEND, and blow a good luck kiss into the ether.

Superstitious? *Moi*? Probably, but if it works then why not do it? It's a bit like a footballer always putting his left sock on first, or a cyclist eating the same meal before every big race.

Writers know how important that envelope, or email attachment, is to them. If they could cast spells then they probably would. If you had a magic wand wouldn't you wave it over each and every piece of work you sent out? But these things are best performed in the privacy of one's own home so kiss your baby before leaving the house.

## Don't expect to sell the film rights

It's what new writers think will happen. And it may, so do keep the intention firmly in mind.

## Letting go

Many writers never send their work out and I can sympathise. Many years ago my knees would knock at the thought of sending a story, article or whatever out into the world.

Letting go (posting or emailing) means that your work is finally on its way to be judged. Will it be good enough for publication? Or is it not up to scratch? Dropping it through that slot means that sooner or later you will find out. It's not an easy thing to do and I have known a few good writers who sadly never reached that stage. Threats to break into their houses at night, steal their work and send it out on their behalf didn't work either.

When my first piece of work was submitted I consoled myself with the fact that my chosen editor would not know me from Adam, or Eve. He wouldn't see my name and picture me as he read my work. Yet why shouldn't he see me? Realisation dawned that I could see him.

He was stout and balding. I saw him going home from the office, letting himself into his house. He sat down to dinner with his wife and made a grab for the Merlot. Pouring himself a large glass he took a swig and, over the sausage and chips said, 'Am I glad to be home, dear. You'd never believe the rubbish I've read today. An illiterate housewife sent me pages and pages of ****. (Sorry dear. I'll put a pound in the swear box.) It was so **** boring. (Sorry, sweetie, two pounds.) I should write and tell her to sell the computer and buy a knitting machine.'

But the more I sent out the more my confidence grew, and so will yours. That editor might love your offering. It could be, 'Wow, darling, have I got news for you. Give the sausages to the dog. We're going out to celebrate. Today I discovered a genius.'

Hang on to that thought.

## Who to trust

When you show your work to someone and ask them what they think, make sure that particular someone can be trusted.

Would you show a broken tooth to a hairdresser? No. Would you take your ingrowing toe-nail to a television repair man? No. So why would you ask for an opinion on your work from your favourite aunt who's won prizes for cake-making, or a neighbour whose gift is growing the largest carrots in the county? Instead, hand it over to someone who knows about writing, who knows about the business, and who can give you some unbiased advice. You may have to pay for an expert's opinion but it will be worth it.

## Rich and famous

Non-writers believe writers are rich. This is because they read newspaper reports about yet another waitress who has penned a masterpiece and had more zeros on the end of their advance than hot dinners they've delivered to tables.

The truth is that these stories make the headline simply because they are so unusual.

Worse is the fact that many would-be writers believe the same thing, that all you need to do is write one half-decent novel and you'll never need to work again.

Real writers know all this is complete nonsense and that writing is a job and can actually be hard work. Those who still have big dreams know that it's not impossible to get those huge advances; nevertheless most of us have to learn our craft and work hard for years in order to become an overnight success.

## What do you do?

A non-writer will ask what you do for a profession and, on being told you write, will immediately ask if they should have heard of you. Non-writers (and even non-readers) think they should know your name if you are a halfway decent author.

Don't let them put you down. What you need to remember is that these non-writers, when asked to name ten authors, will struggle and, if they do manage it, half the list will be deceased. If you don't believe me, try it next time you're asked that dreaded question.

## I'm a writer

I must be. Look at me. I'm wearing a hat with a veil and my cigarette is in a long holder.

That's a true description of a writer from the 1950s.

What does a writer look like anyway? We can wear silly hats and ridiculous waistcoats – it's expected of us (especially poets). The public expect us to be a little on the eccentric side. You can have a trade-mark, like Jane Wenham-Jones's multi-coloured hair. But don't overdo it. Dressing like the public's conception of a writer is probably not a good look.

## Invent an aunt

I don't understand what genetic engineers or astrophysicists do. The jobs sound very grand and these people are undoubtedly left alone to carry on their work in peace. As are dustmen, secretaries and bus-drivers. Have you ever suggested to your bin-man that he might like to leave the rubbish and go out for lunch with you? Of course not. Do you ever phone a friend and suggest she forgets the invoices she's supposed to be sending out and accompanies you on a day's shopping instead? Rarely.

So, why do non-writers expect us to dump our work and join them for an afternoon matinee or a jaunt into town? Isn't our work important? The answer is yes, it is to us, but non-writers cannot get their heads around us not being able to go out because we have a story/article/chapter to finish.

'I'm sorry I can't come for coffee because my heroine's sitting on an upturned tombstone and I can't possibly leave her there,' will mean nothing to them.

'My deadline for this article is tomorrow,' will get a response such as, 'You can do it tonight then, can't you?'

How do you escape this dilemma without losing friends?

Invent an aunt. Make her an aged, non-driving invalid. Give her a chronic illness, something which requires regular hospital appointments. She could also have unexpected ailments at times to suit you.

Doesn't this sound better? 'I'd love to come with you but unfortunately Great-Auntie Mabel's got to see the bunion specialist and *needs* me to take her.'

To non-writing friends, a sick aunt is a valid excuse. Writing isn't.

## Passion

You need passion in this job. Be passionate about your writing whether it's a 25-word letter to the local paper or a 500,000-word novel.

## Will they steal my idea?

It's a new writer's fear. Ideas have no copyright. Just because you have a brilliant idea it doesn't mean that no-one else has thought of it.

Keep that wonderful idea for a story/poem/article to yourself. If you're afraid that someone will steal it do write it sooner rather than later. Ideas often come from what is happening in the world around us so you won't be the only one concentrating on a plane crash or a child abduction. Get writing and hope you'll be the first to get your idea out there.

I'd like to think that writers' moral standards were high enough that no-one stole ideas from others but I'm not that naïve. It may happen sometimes.

## Will they steal my story?

One of my early stories was called *Sunday Tea* – a girl taking her boyfriend home for the first time was worried how he might react to her zany mother. Two months after publication I saw *my* story in another teen magazine. This time it was set at Bonfire Night. My immediate reaction was to shout, 'She's stolen my idea.' And I did. I also allowed this 'crime' to play on my mind for ages until I finally realised that the gap between the stories appearing wasn't long enough for my idea to have been stolen. Two writers had chosen the same subject. Let's face it, how many mothers are out there with teenage daughters? Any one of them could have written it or recounted the experience to a friend who wrote.

## Silence and solitude?

If you love silence and solitude then you are in the right business when it comes to writing. Most writers need both. Some work best when the house is silent and empty. Others can put up with noise and interruptions but they are either parents of young children or they have worked in a noisy newspaper office.

## Party animal?

If you like noise, music, drink and partying then you're in the right business when it comes to selling your books. You'll need to get out there and socialise, chat and sell, sell, sell.

## Train yourself

Train yourself to look for ideas and to ask *what if?*

See the baby in the buggy? What's he going to do over the next eighty years?

See the old lady getting on the bus? What's she been doing for the past eighty years?

See the couple holding hands? See the couple arguing? Who are they? What's going to happen to them?

Witnessed an accident? Note the details in case you ever need to write about one, or need to write about witnessing one.

Every person you meet is a potential character. Every place you visit is a potential location. Every problem you hear is a potential plot.

**EXERCISE – New words**
**Every morning pick up a dictionary and leaf through it until you find a new word. Use that word several times during the day.**

**Instead of a dictionary try a Thesaurus or Foyle's Philavery, a treasury of unusual words. (Philavery – an idiosyncratic collection of uncommon and pleasing words.)**

**Words are the tools of a writer so we need to keep adding to our collection though we do not need to show off by using long and complicated words that our readers won't understand.**

## A leg up

When I began writing I was so grateful for any little tip, any scrap of praise or the slightest bit of encouragement from other writers who were further along the writing path than I was.

Thank you R. T. Plumb. Roy told me I had a passion for words and encouraged me. We all need encouragement.

Remember what it felt like when you first started out on the writing path? You probably felt lost and needed that guidance, wherever or whoever it came from. Now, perhaps you have some published work to your name, a few competition successes, or a book contract in your hand. Don't forget what those early days were like and remember to always help someone who is behind you on the writing path.

## Starving in a garret

Don't give up the day job. It will sustain you until you can live by your writing. Starving in a garret isn't really romantic, and even garrets cost a small fortune in rent these days.

## The other books

When you begin to make money, keep receipts for absolutely everything. You'll be able to claim them as expenses against your tax bill.

# 2

# The clock is ticking

## I don't have time

How many times have you said this? So many wannabe writers complain about lack of time but we can all glean a few minutes here and there.

I'm not good at waiting for things – people, appointments, buses, taxis ... Find the waiting time in your life and fill it with writing. Doctors and dentists' waiting rooms offer ancient magazines with which to pass the time. You could write instead. Get out a pen and paper and make notes. Add a few sentences to your work in progress. Grab those waiting minutes that seem like hours when you are leaning against a bus stop or perched on a bench on a railway station. Once you're writing the time will appear to pass more quickly. In fact you may become unaware of time passing altogether.

Use that waiting time wisely. I knew an elderly lady who had beautiful upper arms. When asked how she managed to keep her arms like that she told me that every time she switched on the kettle she would do arm-tightening exercises while she waited for the water to boil. If waiting for a kettle to boil can do that for her imagine what it could do for your output.

In future, whenever you are waiting, whatever it is for, pick up a pen and get writing instead.

## Write, right now

When I tell anyone that I am a writer they inevitably say they want to write/are going to write one day and then the excuses for not having written get rolled out.

## Too busy

Never think you are too busy to write. Learn to delegate jobs, gardening, shopping and housework. Or forget housework completely. I am assured that four days and four weeks of dust looks exactly the same. If it bothers you pay someone to dust for you. Delegate any work you don't want to do. If you really want to write you'll make the time. Real writers do.

## Too stupid

A long time ago my very first book sold to the first publisher I sent it to. Then I had doubts. This was a fluke. I wasn't clever enough to be a writer. I had no qualifications, no letters after my name. I'd never even been to university. I was too stupid to write. But there was my book – proof that I had either fooled a publisher or that I wasn't as stupid as that little voice kept telling me. Either way I decided to write again. If I could sell more work then I wasn't stupid. Hey, guess what? I'm clever! It's official because I've been writing words and selling them ever since.

Never think you are too stupid to write. Each of us has something to say. Say it and gain confidence.

## Too young

Some ancient Truth said that a writer needed to have lived for at least forty years before they knew enough about life and had enough experience in order to write. Fiddlesticks! Poppycock! Balderdash! Everyone has something to say and there have been, are, and will be plenty of young writers. Younger than forty. Younger than thirty. Younger … you get the idea. Adam Millward sold his first short story to a women's magazine when he was only fourteen years young.

Never think you are too young to write. Start now and accumulate experience.

## Too old

So what if you've left writing until you're retired? What an amazing wealth of experience you now have in your memory banks. What incredible stories and wisdom you have collected over those years. Now is the time to take up writing as a hobby to enjoy, or get serious – think of it as your next career. Imagine becoming a best-selling author and making your grand-children/great-grandchildren proud.

With age comes experience, and success later in life tastes sweeter.

## Making holes

'There's no point in starting.' 'There's not enough time.' Have you ever been guilty of saying something like that? I have. Do you think you need a whole empty morning so that you can begin a project? Or perhaps you decide to put it off because there's never enough time and you turn to something that can be completed in an hour or two instead.

It was a comment by Clare Law (www.threebeautifulthings. blogspot.com) that had an effect on my writing and how I thought about time.

On her blog, she said, 'Even half an hour makes a hole in this work.'

Thanks to that I discovered that half an hour of working on something large, like a book/novel, does indeed make a hole and all those holes are adding up to thousands of words.

Go, make a hole.

## Finding time

Finding time means being selfish, putting yourself first and making your writing priority. It can take a long time to learn that one and it's not as selfish as it sounds. Making time to write will make you happier and that will have a knock-on effect on everyone around you.

The reality is that unless you look for time you'll never find any.

## Picking raspberries

How about thinking of minutes as being like raspberries? There are never enough in one place so you have to wander along picking and plucking until you have a lovely big bowl-full.

Now try plucking minutes instead of fruit. Get up ten, twenty, thirty minutes earlier. Stay up ten, twenty, thirty minutes later. Gain half an hour by giving up a soap. Have you found an hour's worth yet? Use that time to write in.

## Saving more minutes

Don't spend valuable time by sitting down to write and then re-arranging the desk, sipping tea and staring out of the window before you begin. Know exactly what you are going to work on before you sit down to work.

## Working but not writing

It's very easy to tell yourself that you've done a good day's work yet you haven't written a word. Writing is not just putting words on the screen, or paper. There is the admin to do too. There are emails to reply to, comments to make on Facebook. Tweets to compose. Invoices to send out. Proposals to put together. Editors to chase. You may be reading up on your subject, doing a bit of research, tidying your desk, attacking that filing, talking about writing ...

It's all writing related. (I'm not even going to include here the housework, shopping and myriad other jobs we all need to tackle.)

It's very easy to allow yourself to believe that all this writing related stuff constitutes a good writing day but, be honest with yourself, does it really?

No. It's not getting your novel closer to the end. It's not getting that article or short story written.

Yes, all that writing related stuff needs to be done but start allocating it to later in the day when your creative stint is over. Make sure you write first, then tackle the writing related jobs afterwards. Think how good you'll feel then. The late, great Keith Waterhouse famously said, 'One of the pleasures about writing for a living is having written.' Make sure you've written. Enjoy that pleasant feeling.

## New Year writing resolutions

Years ago my writing group came up with a good idea. All the members wrote down their writing resolutions and handed them over to the Secretary during the first meeting of the new year. They weren't read. Oh, no! They were sealed in an envelope and stored in a safe place until the final meeting of the year and then, amidst much grumbling and some elation, the envelope was ceremoniously opened and the resolutions read out loud.

Writers were congratulated on achieving what they had set out to do, or encouraged to try harder the following year. Occasionally one or two would list their excuses for not sticking to their resolutions and another couple would always avoid that particular meeting so they didn't need to explain themselves.

On the whole it worked well for most of the group and it was all carried out in a good-natured way. Please feel free to steal that idea and, if you don't belong to a group, perhaps you could swap resolutions with a writing friend and make a date for coffee and the grand opening in late December.

EXERCISE – Any time resolutions
You don't need a new year for resolutions. Today will do. Any day will do. Don't ask if this is the *year* in which you actually sit down and write your novel/sell more stories and articles/get into print for the first time. You can start the work today. You can continue it tomorrow. You don't need to wait for a specific day to begin. You need to do it now.

# 3

# Growing confidence

## I'm a believer

Once upon a time, many years ago, I was told by a wizard (i.e. a person in authority) that I was lazy. This person told me many times and in the end I believed it. For years afterwards the spell remained strong. I was lazy. That was my belief.

One day a prince came along, as they do in all the best fairy stories. The prince told me, 'No way are you lazy. You're always busy doing things, writing, looking after the family. Who told you that you were lazy? And why did you buy into that belief?'

So I asked myself those questions and gave myself the answers and began believing I was good and hard-working. Now I no longer buy into anything I don't want to. The spell has been broken. Permanently.

Make sure you are not under a spell. If someone tells you that you are lazy, can't write, have no talent, you don't have to believe it. The choice is yours.

## Believe in yourself

It can be difficult at times. For instance, when people ask if they should know your name. When relatives ask when your big breakthrough is due. When you sit staring at the screen and no words come. When you read a great book and know you'll never write one just as good.

These are the times when you have to get a grip. Ignore the voice in your head telling you that you are not good enough. Laugh with your relatives and friends and tell them anytime soon.

Tell yourself you can do it and then get on with it. As Mike Dooley once said in one of his daily messages from the Universe,

'Be still. Stop thinking. Feel. Take action. Visualise. Repeat.' (see www.tut.com)

## Act As If

'I don't have much confidence in my writing. You seem to have oodles of it,' a creative writing student had added at the end of her assignment.

*If only you knew*, I thought and set about writing an honest reply. Want to know what it was?

I wrote, 'Confidence? I don't have oodles but I pretend to. Before doing a talk or workshop it's a case of chin up, bust out, stomach in, and smile. It works and it's called the *As If Principle*. If you act *as if* you are something then you are more likely to become it.'

This theory works in life as well as writing. Act like a winner and you can become one. Feeling tired? Your shoulders are drooping and your feet shuffling? Act as if you are filled with energy. Lift those shoulders, let those feet dance. Now how do you feel?

It's all about acting a part.

Still lacking confidence? At a public reading I watched several supremely self-assured writers take the stage and loudly read their work with confidence. One even told the audience how much they were about to enjoy his poem. (Yawn.) I was almost asleep when an elderly lady took her place centre stage. She was visibly shaking and, in a trembling voice, read out the best piece of the night. She lacked confidence but not talent. The two don't necessarily go together.

## The biggest problem

'What would you like me to talk about?' I asked the leader of the writing group.

'My students reckon their biggest problem is lack of confidence and self-belief,' was the reply. 'I'm sure they think there's a magical point at which they will suddenly feel good enough despite me telling them that with most people that doesn't happen. You just have to believe you're good enough and keep trying if the first attempt at something doesn't work.'

I began that particular talk by telling these creative writing students how I had been asked to leave school a year early 'so that the rest of the class could concentrate'. I went on to inform them that for years I believed that every piece of my writing accepted for publication was a fluke. How I had dreams of being found out. That someone would tap me on the shoulder and tell me that I wasn't a real writer. That I was bluffing my way through life pretending.

Then someone I greatly admired told me, that along with lots of other writers, she felt the same way. Lots of us do but we all carry on and don't let those negative thoughts get in the way of our work. Writing can be difficult. No-one in any other profession gets knocked back as often and as uncaringly as we do.

Confidence is all about being positive and learning to believe in yourself.

**EXERCISE – Boosting confidence**
**You will need a large sheet of stiff card, some glue, coloured paper, a pair of scissors, felt-tip pens and some sticky-backed plastic. Actually I'm joking about the last item, but not about the rest. You are going to make an Ego Booster Board (if you feel so inclined).**

**Glue a photo of yourself at the top. Now photocopy any book jackets, banners from magazines your work has appeared in, certificates from writing competitions etc. Artistically arrange them and then stick them on the board. Finally, write a bit about your successes, making it sound really good. Do it on pretty coloured paper and stick that to the board too.**

**Put this in a prominent place and when you feel low take a**

good look at it and remind yourself that you have achieved before so there's no reason why you can't do the same again.

## Our unique voice

I once took over a class which had been led by an academic who had set homework such as *write a story in the style of Jane Austen*. The entire class was a joy to teach. Each student had obviously learned the techniques of writing but few had discovered their own style. They were merely copying that of respected but dead authors. Writing is all about finding your own voice, your own style.

Admire other writers. Study their styles but be yourself.

## Never say no

Whenever you are asked to write, and promised payment, even if it's an article in a foreign language, say yes. Worry later. On second thoughts, never worry. Simply tell yourself, 'I can do this!'

When you are starting out, don't be too picky. Take whatever comes along. You never know what it might lead to. The time to be more selective is when you have plenty of work coming in and can afford to pick and choose.

Stepping out of your comfort zone needn't be a frightening prospect. You never know what you can do until you try it. Give it your best shot and you may surprise yourself.

## Brains are funny things

How often do we put something in a story and only know later why we did so? It's something beyond what's rational. I didn't fully realise this until I had a go at writing a novel. It happened in exactly the way many writers describe. My characters took on lives of their own and refused to do what they were supposed to do. One insisted on doing something totally unexpected so I thought I'd go back in the story and add a clue as to what was going to happen later. And what happened? My clue was already there. It was as if my brain had put it there without me realising.

Now, had I lost the plot? I hung on to what a friend had told me years ago – 'You're too scatty to go batty' and asked other writers if they'd experienced something similar. Yes, they had.

Novelist and creative writing tutor, Sue Johnson, told me, 'When I was working on revisions to my second novel, *The Yellow Silk Dress*, I woke one morning convinced that I needed to add more detail to a scene set in Paris. When I switched on the computer and went to that chapter, it was all there, complete with old-fashioned lift, wrought iron balcony and the smell of coffee with chicory. I had no recollection of writing it!'

And Sue Houghton confirmed I wasn't losing the plot. 'I had a male character,' she said, 'who was a smoker and decided to have him try to give up, hence a possible reason for his moodiness towards my heroine. I went back through my first few chapters only to find my heroine had been carrying smokers' patches in her handbag all along. I have no idea how they got there but it saved me writing in a scene.'

And there we have it. The proof that I'm as sane as any other writer.

Consider yourself sane and trust your brain to do some of that background work for you. It probably has.

## More proof

Need more proof about the mysterious workings of writers' brains?

Prolific writer, Teresa Ashby, confirmed that, 'Yes, I've experienced that! I've been well into a story and then thought that something needed to have happened earlier for this to happen, then when I've gone back to write it in, it's already there. Quite spooky really. It's as if I've written on autopilot. Also I have been aware of putting something in, only to become aware of why much later. And another thing, I've also read published stories of mine and thought, "I wish I'd thought to put that bit in," thinking the editor had done it, only to check my original and find I had put it in. It's like you get taken over isn't it?'

Novelist Jane Jackson has more to say on the subject. 'When this happens to me I praise my subconscious for remembering even when my mind was distracted by other stuff. I read somewhere, a long time ago, that your subconscious takes what you say literally, and believes what you tell it. So if you tell yourself, "I'm an idiot" or "I can't remember things" it will believe you and you will have created a self-fulfilling prophecy. So when I've had a panic about going back and putting something vital in that I thought I'd forgotten, then find it's already there, I give myself a pat on the back for remembering that it was important, and another pat on the back for having already done it. We demand a huge amount of ourselves, so it's not surprising if, now and again, our brains have a kind of stutter. Be kind to yourself, offer yourself praise instead of a scolding, and it will quickly settle down.'

## Human or alien?

My hands shook. My knees dipped. I almost curtseyed. No, it wasn't the queen in front of me. It was one of my favourite authors. I had put this woman on a pedestal for years – a goddess whose words transported readers into the past. Yet here she was, asking me what I wrote as if we were equals. And there was I stuttering a reply, trying to tell her how much joy she had given me through her books.

This famous writer was a normal human-being. And she was friendly and helpful.

The lesson is – approach that writer you have worshipped. Speak to them. Check out they are human ... no different from you.

## That extrovert friend

If you are too timid to approach your writing hero/heroine then get your extrovert friend to do it for you. Ask them to go and speak to them and then you can wander nonchalantly up and join in the conversation.

If you haven't got an extrovert friend, it's time you found one.

## Little acorns

The first words I ever sold netted me £2. It was for a letters page in a magazine. I photocopied the cheque.

That letter gave me the confidence to approach a local newspaper and tell them I was a freelance writer. A slight exaggeration but they gave me assignments which gave me the courage to send out work to magazines. You could say *from little acorns* ...

We can't all come up with a best-selling novel at our first attempt so why not try my 'little acorn' method? Being successful in a small way, such as seeing a letter or household tip in print, can be the bottom rung on your ladder to success.

And don't forget – the first time you receive money for something you have written is a wonderful occasion. Photocopy the cheque or the bank statement. Print out the acceptance email or frame the letter. Put them on view so when doubt creeps in you can see the proof, right there in front of you, that you are a writer.

## Success is doing. Not wishing.

'Success is doing. Not wishing.' That's written above my desk, along with a lot of other little mantras to keep me on the straight and narrow.

It's easy to sit down with a cuppa and slip into a dream about seeing your work in print or being a best-selling author. *I want to be a writer* is easy to say, lovely to dream about and simple to wish for but in order to achieve it you need to **do** something.

You learn. You practise. You decide exactly what you want to write.

Learning should be fun. There are books to buy or borrow, courses to enrol on, classes to attend, talks to go to, workshops to join, other writers and wannabes to meet and exchange information and ideas with.

Decide which options are the best for you. Which ones would you enjoy and be able to manage? It's no use signing up for a creative writing class twenty miles away if you don't drive and there's no public transport. Be sensible. Select what is achievable. If you can't get to a class, sign up for a correspondence course instead. Make a list of the things you could **do** to be successful and try to **do** something every day to take you nearer to your goal.

**EXERCISE – Your worst nightmare**
**What is your worst nightmare? Or what's that phobia you struggle with? Write about them. As writers we need to tackle the difficult stuff, the uncomfortable subjects. They can't always be avoided.**

**Take a deep breath, then write for five minutes on why you can't touch buttons (my particular phobia) or can't dispose of spiders, or have to run away from clowns. Your fear could shine through in your writing so if you put this into a piece of fiction it would shine through to the publisher.**

**Yes, it's difficult. No-one said it would be easy. You have to tackle the hard stuff in order to call yourself a writer.**

## Making changes

'I was wondering if you'd make a few changes to a story you sent us,' he said. 'He' being a fiction editor with a women's magazine.

'Of course,' I said.

Making changes is a lesson that has to be learned. We may not like the changes. Many new writers resent being asked to make any changes to their masterpiece and if those changes have been made by an editor and they see something slightly different from their original in the print version they wail, 'My title's been changed.' Or, 'My characters' names have been changed.' Or, 'There's a whole paragraph missing.'

You know the old adage about the customer always being right? In publishing it's normally a case of the editor being right.

I know of well-established writers being asked to make changes to their work and when they do so they admit that their work is all the better for it.

I also know of a writer whose story was rejected but it sold when sent to a foreign market. That writer, Simon Whaley, copied the changes the editor had made and sent the changed story out again here. It was accepted. Could this be proof that the editor knows best?

## Get on with it

It was my first day working in a newspaper office. The editor gave me a pile of letters containing news from various groups. My job was to turn them into useable prose. I read the first and sat back to consider how to construct my news item. The editor prodded me in the back. 'What are you doing?' he asked. 'Thinking about it,' I told him. And then he told me how reporters worked. There isn't the luxury of thinking time. You get on with it and get it right first time. On a small paper like his – four staff including advertising – you also wrote quickly. Now, when I'm sitting struggling over a piece of work, I remember that prod in the back and get on with it.

So, you out there, stop dithering and Get On With It.

**EXERCISE – Just do it**
**The runner puts on his shoes and runs. The painter picks up a brush and goes for that paper/canvas. If you want to be a writer you'd best get writing. You need to be doing it, not thinking about it or thinking about doing it one day.**

**Stop reading this and go pick up a pen and some paper.**

Write down whatever comes into your head. Write down your writing aspirations. Get working. Get writing. No excuses now. Just do it.

# 4

# Good ideas

### Change the mind-set

Get rid of negative thoughts and beliefs. Watch your words. Never tell yourself, 'I'm not good/clever enough.' Change it to 'I am good. I am clever. I can do it.'

### Change the time

So many writers say that mornings are their best time. I wonder if they've ever tried any other time. Just as an experiment, try writing tomorrow afternoon, tonight, just before you go to bed or as soon as you wake. Try a different time of the day and see if something amazing happens.

### Change the place

If you're going to be changing the time you write, how about going the whole hog and changing the place too. I had always written in my room, at my desk. Then we bought a motorhome and began travelling around the coast of Britain. At first I told myself I couldn't write because I wasn't in my writing place. Finally I told myself to get over it and began writing on camp-sites, on beaches, on the top of hills. It was a sort of picnic writing. If you can eat anywhere, as in a picnic, then there's no reason why you can't write anywhere.

### Write it down

Keep notebooks and pens with you at all times. We all tell ourselves we'll remember that incredible idea for a story or article but wonderful ideas can pop out of the mind as easily and quickly as they pop in.

Ideas often surface when we're in the wrong place. It can be difficult to stop and make notes whilst riding a bike or making pastry so sometimes we have to rely on memory, or keep chanting that title, sentence or plot until it can be committed to paper.

There's a story about Roald Dahl not having anything to write with when Charlie and The Chocolate Factory burst into his head. This was in the days before mobile phones so he couldn't phone home and leave himself a message. He is said to have stopped his car, got out and scribbled his idea in the dust on the boot.

Read any good cars lately?

**EXERCISE – Open me**
**Buy a little notebook. Make sure its cover appeals to you as you're going to be using it a lot.**

**Now, whenever you see a quote that inspires you, write it in your notebook. There are days when confidence or inspiration deserts us and that's when you open your notebook and have a read.**

**Mine began with a quote from Molière followed by one from Samuel Smiles. I kept adding and kept reading.**

**My collection is still being added to. That book is like a tiny friend with a big attitude. Start yours right now.**

## Night ideas I

It's horrible when writers wake in the night with a brilliant idea, make a huge effort to get out of bed to write it down and, in the morning, discover it's rubbish. It's even worse if you break your toe in the process of getting up to write your notes. (Always turn on the lights in order to avoid chair legs.)

Please remember that those wonderful ideas you had in the early hours when you couldn't be bothered to get out of bed and there was no paper or pen on the bedside table, were undoubtedly rubbish.

# Night ideas 2

On the other hand ... those ideas that come to you in the middle of the night might be wonderful. They may need a little more thinking through – we're never at our best when half asleep. Make sure you capture them on paper. Always keep pen and paper by the bed. Make sure it's there when you get into bed. Someone might have borrowed it during the day.

## Stuck? Solution 1

Got a problem with the plot? Written yourself into a corner?

Many years ago I was given some advice by R. T. Plumb, a novelist and supplier of over forty short stories to BBC Radio 4. 'Have some cheese and pickles before going to bed,' he told me. 'They'll keep you awake all night and you'll have solved the problem by morning.'

Cheese and pickles were his favourite late-night snack. He knew what the effect would be but made use of it. Instead of complaining about indigestion, he would work out his writing problems. If you have a penchant for hard-to-digest food late at night then this could work for you.

## Stuck? Solution 2

Got a problem with the plot? Written yourself into a corner? Before you drop off to sleep ask yourself how to get out of it, then trust yourself and your intuition. You'll have solved the problem by morning.

It may take a bit of practice but stop being negative. Don't tell yourself it can't work, won't work. We only use a third of our brains so why can't the remainder be capable of solving a few problems. Trust!

## Stuck? Solution 3

You can learn how to do this one too. Remember, it's amazing how the brain works without us consciously using it.

Put a note under your pillow. What do you write in this note? You write down your problem. 'What happens next?'

And, if you're stuck for a short story idea, write three items on your note. 'Snow, darkness, friends.'

Give it a kiss. Or hold it and ask your brain, the Universe, the Muse, whatever turns you on, to supply you with an answer. Pop it under your pillow. Get your eight hours, six hours, whatever, and wake with the answer in your head.

Try it. Practise often and the results keep coming.

## Read your genre

I've met writers who want to have a short story in a women's magazine but freely admit to never reading one. 'Not my sort of thing,' they say.

If you admit to never reading the genre you are writing for then you are not doing your job properly. Read and study, whether it be crime, sci-fi, Westerns, erotica, romance or women's magazines.

**EXERCISE – Start an ideas box**
**First find a box. Plain cardboard will do, or one of those plastic storage boxes. Now start filling it with ideas. Find some magazines and newspapers and, from them, cut out any pictures that interest you. Pictures of people may turn out to be characters in your novel or short story. Pictures of places, buildings, scenery can be used as a setting – a bluebell wood, an old cottage, an exotic beach. Snip out bits of articles that might spark an idea for something similar. Turn to the Agony Aunt's page. Many are the times that other people's problems have become the basis for a short story of mine.**

## Caring for an ideas box

An ideas box should grow and shrink as you add new ideas or remove old ones and use them.

To keep your box thriving add anything thought-provoking, interesting or inspirational. Keep adding pictures, photos and postcards. Don't rush this process. In hindsight I think my box was rushed, the main motive being to make it look full, interesting and bulging with, well … ideas.

## Feeding an ideas box

Whenever you get an idea jot it down on a piece of paper and add it to your box. Whenever you find an interesting fact add it to your box. Dream up a dozen opening lines for stories and add them. Dream up a dozen closing lines for stories and add them too. To keep your box healthy, make sure that you sift through its contents at regular intervals. If you can't think what to write then open your box and be inspired.

## Covering letters

When sending out work is it a good idea to include a covering letter? Let's look at it this way. What are you going to say in one if you are submitting a short story?

'This is a story called *If at First You Don't Succeed*. It's 1000 words long. I hope you like it.'

What else is there to say? The editor will see what the title is because it will be on your cover sheet, along with the length and all your contact details. She has a pile of stories to get through. Does she need the same number of letters to read too, especially if they don't actually say anything of importance?

Some newbies may think they need to add an explanation about some event in their story. 'The facts in this story are correct. Maggots do turn into flies and this is what caused the accident in the angler's car.' No! Most people would know this and, if they didn't, it should be explained in the story. If a story needs explaining in a covering letter then it's not a good story. (In my youth I sent that maggot information to an editor in a letter. My story was rejected.)

A good suitable story will make it every time, unless it's in a tiny font and coloured ink. I reckon anyone with half a brain would throw one of those out without reading it. As a competition judge, I have.

## Yes, yes, yes
Avoid repetition, unless it's for deliberate effect. You can spot the unintended repetition of words by reading work aloud.

## Bulls-eye
Set yourself a target and stick to it. It's been said many times – and it's true – if you write only one page a day you'll have a novel in a year's time. And once you start writing you'll probably do more than a page

## Reached the star?
When you achieve your writing ambition make another one. Always have a writing ambition. And remember you're never too old to have a new dream.

## Read books twice?
I used to tell learner writers to read books twice. The first time for the sheer pleasure, the second time for analysis. Now I realise there's not enough time to read a book twice. (Okay. I do have favourites that are returned to, especially in times of illness when curling up in bed with a good book is the best cure and you remember that the good book you want is a childhood favourite, or that certain one you indulge in every year or so.)

Now, because there are too many books to read and not enough time, I've changed the tune. Now my advice is to read the first time for the pleasure of it and then return to the passages that made you laugh, or cry. Those paragraphs or pages that stirred some strong emotion in you, whether it was joy, pity, disgust, excitement ... Check out how that brilliant writer achieved this. How did they make you laugh or cry? How did they stir your emotions. It's a magical thing to be able to do using only words. The answer is there in the right choice of words, the length of the sentences, and the beauty of the rhythm. And you can learn from it.

## Got to be in it to win it

Want to win the lottery? Buy a ticket. As the saying goes, you've got to be in it to win it. The same goes for writing competitions. A win looks great on the old Writing CV. Or being placed, or being long-listed or short-listed or a runner-up, or highly commended.

Entering writing competitions gives you experience. You send your work out into the big wide world. You have to write to a certain length and to complete your work by the closing date – your deadline. You have to stick to certain rules. If they say 1500 words maximum, they mean it. If they want double spacing and white paper, use double spacing and white paper. The rules usually say that your name should not be in your manuscript. Make sure it isn't. If you break the rules you may not get as far as being judged and you'll have wasted your entry fee.

Some competitions offer critiques of the entries you send in. Take advantage of any critique offered. It's good to know what strangers think of your work.

Enter one competition a year, or one a month, but make sure they are the real thing. There are bad ones. The organisers tell everyone they're a winner and then ask for an extortionate sum to buy the anthology that their work appears in. 'Why not buy extras for friends and family?' they ask. And that's what new writers often do. These companies have been known to target schools too. Make sure you don't part with your money for something that is pure vanity.

## Reality versus online

Visit your local library and bookshops regularly. They need your support and, in exchange, they will offer you real books that you can hold, leaf through, smell. A library is also a real environment. There will be people there; humans who are talking, reading, searching the shelves. There may be a coffee shop where overheard conversations (ideas) are taking place and you are free to listen in to them. There may be events to attend. Watch the children being read to and note their reactions. Visit a class on creative writing. Check out the information board to see what's happening in your area. Libraries aren't just books. They are buildings filled with ideas.

Never pass a bricks and mortar bookshop. They too are places of inspiration and information. Check out what's selling and what isn't. Go along those shelves like a vacuum cleaner searching out dust, only you will be looking for gold dust. Search for the book that will light your world, that unheard of author who will become a new favourite. And remember, you'll want that bookshop on your side when you have your first signing there.

## Librarian/friend

Make friends with your librarian. These are knowledgeable people. They know which books are being borrowed at an amazing rate. They know which books parents pick up for their children and which the kids choose for themselves. They can guide you to the shelf that holds that gem of information you spent half an hour searching for and couldn't find.

## Don't lean back

Eavesdropping is part of a writer's life but don't lean too far back in your chair when listening to conversation at the next table in a restaurant. You might fall and hurt yourself.

I once sat in a café at a table next to several elderly ladies who were having a good chat. Out came my notebook and down went their remarks. 'She's a lovely girl but ...' and they all nodded and didn't complete the sentence. It was up to me, the writer, to come up with the reason she wasn't completely lovely. And later, 'It's in the boot of my car but I don't like to get it out while there are people around.' Wow! What on earth could it be?

These ladies were quite loud and I didn't need to lean in closer. I came home with a page filled with their quotes, several of which became the inspiration for short stories.

Next time you are in a restaurant or café, position yourself so that you can tune in to the customers around you. And if you do need to lean back, please take care. More than one writer has come a cropper.

## Chocolate wrappings not included

Keep every scrap of paper and every little note you use while writing your novel. You never know what you may need later.

A large pretty basket or plain old black bin-bag will hold all the discarded scraps of useless prose. All those ideas which don't can be dropped into the waste which may not turn out to be waste after all. At some point in your work you may wish you'd never thrown away that scintillating scrap of dialogue. But all is not lost. You can spend a happy hour searching through your discarded bits until you find what you want. You may also discover other discarded bits that have suddenly become valuable contributions. (There's no need to save all your chocolate wrappings unless you plan on turning them into some sort of sculpture which you can wheel in and out of stores when you are signing your books.)

## Keeping schtum

When you're a writer you learn a lot about plots and plotting. It can spoil things for you when you read a book or watch a film. Reading a book is a solitary occupation but, usually, when you watch a film there are other people in the cinema. If you watch it at home you may not be on your own so resist the temptation to tell everyone what the ending will be. The very best books and films are the ones where even good writers are surprised by the outcome and it's a good and plausible one. You just didn't see it coming.

By all means use your writing skills to work out the end result but don't go telling everyone and spoiling it for them. Keep schtum!

## Play truant?

Very few workers take their jobs wherever they go. An accountant does not sit on the beach with his spreadsheets (or whatever an accountant has). The sensible ones switch off their mobile phones too. Maybe it's only writers who take their work with them. Think of all those notepads on beaches, those laptops in hotel rooms.

Now here's a thought. Perhaps those of you who think you should write every day are wrong. You could take some time off. Really take it off. No writing at all. Then return to work refreshed. You don't even need to go away on holiday. You could simply stay out of your writing room for a few days.

The wonderfully witty novelist, Laurie Graham, takes one day off a week and goes out somewhere. She calls it her Sabbath. A regular Sabbath could prevent writers' block, or writers getting stale. Go play truant …

Just a thought.

## There are other magazines available

Spend fifteen minutes staring at the shelves in your local newsagents. Look at all the magazines there, not the ones you usually aim for.

Visit other newsagents, especially if you are somewhere new. If you live deep in the country there are magazines targeted at the farming community and those country-dwellers who have huge gardens and grow all their own vegetables.

If you visit a city newsagent there may be more magazines about cars, finance, travel.

If you always go for a women's magazine, try something completely different instead. Variety is the spice of life and all that.

Writers need new markets and new ideas and by picking up a new-to-you magazine you could find both.

## None of the above

There are magazines covering every subject under the sun and they all have to be filled with words. Someone has to write those words and it could be you. Doll's houses, teddy bears, ships, airplanes, coins, pottery ... the list is endless.

Did you just say you don't know anything about any of the above? Then find out.

A writer I know found an ancient coin under the floorboards of her house. It fascinated her so she visited the library to find out what she could about this coin. It was enough for an article. The article sold. Even better, the editor asked for more work from her. One tiny coin led to several good commissions.

Look out for unusual magazines because you never know what you can write until you try it.

I was once asked to write a property column. What did I know about the subject? Nothing. Did that stop me? No. All you have to do in a situation like that is ask an expert, or several.

# 5

# Working methods

## Be realistic

It's more realistic to aim for 500 words a day than 1500. The first is achievable and you will find that once those 500 are completed you'll be in full flow and can carry on. By the end of your writing session you could have achieved far more than you set out to do and imagine how good you'll feel then. But if you aim high and let yourself down you'll feel bad.

Set a minimum and picture getting way past it.

## The way to work 1

You need to be comfortable in order to work. If you constantly slide towards the front of your seat or have to keep twitching your keyboard into position, or open and close the curtains to keep the sun off your screen, then you are not going to be able to slip into writing mode.

Make sure you have a comfortable chair, a desk at the right height and good light.

## The way to work 2

It's not good for you to sit, eyes on screen, for long periods of time. You need to take regular breaks. Try writing for a specific time, say twenty minutes, twenty-five, half-an-hour, and then get up and stretch for a while. Take a walk in the garden, make a cup of tea. Do something active before you sit down to work again.

Arrange your work area so that certain items are out of reach. Don't consider it annoying when you have to get up and take a few steps in order to reach the telephone, or switch on the printer. Realise that by doing this you are moving, won't get writers' bottom (spreads if you sit on it all day) or pins and needles in your legs from poor circulation because you've not moved for hours. Think of this getting up to reach something, getting up to stretch for something, a sort of mini-work-out.

## Get organised

Establish a routine. If you have to juggle writing with going to work, looking after a home and family then you need to get organised. Finding time to write can be difficult.

Learn to delegate. Hand out jobs to the rest of the family. Know what time you have and when you will have it. Write yourself a timetable and stick to it.

## Stay disorganised

Routines don't work for everyone. Certainly not for me. Those nine-to-five jobs bore me. That is the reason I gave up trying to keep a job and took up writing instead. Okay, some days I faff about and nothing gets done but other days I can knock out the words and only stop when I get hungry. If you are not too organised you will leave a space for surprises to arrive.

## No clocking off

Writers never clock off. They work wherever they are. They meet people, see places, get ideas and inspiration. Then there's the self-promotion, the talks, workshops and maybe even book-signings.

Most people's days hold work, home life, leisure time, sleep time. All these belong in separate compartments.

Writers, however, are always writers, whatever they are doing. When they are cooking a meal, when they are playing golf, when they're with the kids and even when they are sleeping.

## Goof around

Bless Russell Grant, my favourite astrologer. Imagine my joy at being told that Aquarians needed a day off. 'Go, goof around,' he said. While I am doing this a brilliant idea will come to me, according to Mr Grant. This is what can happen when you distract your conscious mind. By doing that your creative mind is allowed freedom.

Ideas always arrive when you least expect them. You're gardening and don't have pen and paper. You're in the middle of the weekly shop. Your conscious mind is not thinking about writing, but your creative one is beavering away, doing its own thing.

Stop thinking about the glitch in your plot and it may well take care of itself.

Take time to goof around.

**EXERCISE – give yourself permission**
**Go and do something completely different. Take a day off and visit a new place. Go see a friend. Goof around.**

## Warm up

Athletes do warm-up exercises before they run, jump or cycle. So how about writers? Some of us will be able to dive in right away and get down to our work in progress while others will need a warm-up. How do you do that? Try answering a few emails, blogging or writing a letter to a friend. The latter is so sweet and quaint.

## Cool down

If you've warmed up to begin with, do you need to cool down when you're finished? You may find yourself slowing down as a session comes to its natural conclusion. You may want to end abruptly, in the middle of a sentence or exciting scene so that you have somewhere to pick up on the following day. Whatever suits you, Writer.

## Leave some juice

If you're on a roll, stop before you write yourself out completely. Twenty-five years ago I left my heroine sitting in a churchyard. She's still there. Don't leave characters sitting still. Leave your plot at an exciting point so that you don't run out of juice.

## Different approach, same results

I was giving a talk on how to write short stories for the women's magazine market. All I could really tell them was how I do it and that can often involve a different technique for each story.

In the back row of this audience sat another published writer. No-one knew who she was even though she had sold several hundred stories. (Writers tend to be anonymous. I once sat next to James Herbert and hadn't a clue who he was.)

As I talked, telling the group how I wrote and how I submitted stories to magazines, the writer at the back kept shaking her head. Afterwards she told me, 'I don't do any of that. I work completely differently to you.' Which only goes to prove that there is no right way of writing a story, novel, article, anything that will definitely sell.

Perhaps we should have done a double act and caused total confusion.

So, is it worth listening to any of us? Yes. New ideas, tips and techniques can work for you. What you have to do is go, listen, learn and take home and practise the bits that suit you.

## The scary way

Many writers will tell you to plan a novel. It makes sense. Everyone needs to know where they are going.

Re-read that last sentence. *Everyone needs to know where they are going.*

Isn't that The End? If you are one of those who don't plan and simply sit each day waiting to see where your story leads you, then you need to trust yourself. With confidence, keep heading towards the end. It's the scariest way of writing but it works. Ray Bradbury said planning was like putting the footprints before the footsteps.

EXERCISE – Making dates

Write down five things you want to achieve. To finish your novel? To complete a short story? To write an article? To interview a celebrity? To enter a writing competition?

Now add a date for each item you want to achieve.

Finish your novel. How about giving yourself twelve months from today? Write the date down by the project.

Complete a short story. By the end of this month? Write down the date next to it.

Write an article. Can you manage that this month as well, or would it be more realistic to put a date for the end of next month? Remember you need time to finish that novel so don't overload yourself.

Interview a celebrity. Do you have one in mind? Do you know how they can be contacted? Until they say yes to being interviewed you'll need to break this one down into bite-sized chunks. Find the celeb. Ask them if they're willing to be interviewed. Find a market to sell the finished project to. Put a date by each. Then put down a date for completing the finished interview.

Enter a writing competition. Do you have a specific one in mind or will any do? If there is a specific one then it will have a closing date. Don't put that date down. Put one much earlier. Competition organisers like to receive entries in plenty of time.

Now those aims are not dreams, they are real and have finishing times. Without a finishing line a runner won't know when to stop. Without a finishing date a writer won't know when to begin and the task can become endless.

## The dreaded E word

Exercise (as in moving about).

Writers do need to take some exercise. I've always used the excuse that I'm a static sort of person and that exercise is dangerous. (Remember how Stephen King was seriously injured whilst out for his daily constitutional?) Now there has been a change of mind brought about by me hobbling around for five minutes after getting up from a writing session. My back protests about lack of use, so now I am risking that daily walk, or doing a bit of gardening, anything that can be classed as Exercise.

The Pomodora Method helps (see Red Tomato Writing later in this chapter) as it means you have to move after twenty-five minutes of writing.

**EXERCISE – Exercise**
**Take five minutes to stretch or run up and down stairs or, if you live in a bungalow, run on the spot. Do it now.**

## Diet

Years ago the stereo-typical writer had a cigarette dangling from his/her lips. Nowadays, rather than empty fag packets, it's more likely to be wrappings from chocolate bars filling the writers' waste-paper basket.

Unfortunately, though it may feel like you've completed a marathon, writing does not use up many calories. Take care over your food consumption. And, if you find yourself beginning to flag, try taking vitamin supplements, especially during the winter months.

## A To Do list

Write out a To Do list. Use a lovely hard-backed notebook. Each Sunday, on the right-hand page, list the writing jobs you want to do. As you tackle and complete each job, cross it off.

On the left-hand page write down notes, thoughts, ideas or

telephone messages. That's your messy page. At the end of the week anything that's not been achieved gets transferred to the next page and you begin all over again.

No-one sees your book so no-one knows how hard you've worked (or how much time you've wasted, but we won't go there).

One writer bravely, or foolishly, writes down what she wants to achieve each month *on her blog*. At the end of each month she tells us all what she has achieved – lots – and what she proposes to get through the following month – lots more. She doesn't have any messages there to say she's dashed off to Devon, on the spur of the minute, or been very easily persuaded to take the afternoon off to wander around shops with a friend. I do both of those things and more.

That is not to say that my friend's method is the right one and mine is wrong. No. We all have to find what suits us and that can change from week to week.

## Work Smarter

Novelist Damian McNicholl once mentioned a method of working called Work Smarter Not Harder.

It's all about getting your project completed in the shortest possible time.

I'm up for that.

Damian asked, 'When you're supposed to be writing, how much time do you spend doing other things? Emailing, surfing the net and writing related jobs should not take up writing time. They're for a separate time.'

When Damian begins a novel he uses the Work Smarter Not Harder method to prepare a comprehensive list of tasks that must be done to complete the project.

'On your calendar you set a time period and insert time slots to write the outline so you'll know the plot and research required. Once that's complete, you set a time period for the research and break it down into various time slots. Add those to your calendar. And then you decide upon a realistic period for writing the first draft and enter that into your calendar, setting targets of where you need to be on the project by various dates. Once you actually begin the writing you need to make sure you're at your desk at the time slot scheduled and you don't leave until you've completed the job that is assigned for that time.'

And there you have it. It's similar to Mike Dooley's advice about taking 'baby steps' (www.tut.com) and to Simon Whaley's given in his new book, *The Positively Productive Writer*. My advice? Don't rush for your diary now, not when you could be writing. Wait until you've written and then devise your plan to work smarter.

You need to be very disciplined for this method to suit you. Everyday distractions have to be ignored otherwise you won't achieve the set goal.

It's not for me but it could work beautifully for you.

## Red Tomato Writing

I'm always up for a new method of writing and recently bought a kitchen timer in the shape of a red tomato. I set it for twenty-five minutes and have to work for that time. Then I get a five-minute break. Novelist Ben Kane told me about it in an interview. It works for him and now for me too. It's called the Pomodora Method because *pomodora* is Italian for tomato and that's the shape of the timer. After four Pomodoras (twenty-five minutes of undisturbed writing) you take a longer break. The idea is that the brain gets tired after that length of time and stops working at its best.

It's slightly more complex than I cover here and worth taking a look at. See www.pomodorotechnique.com if you want to know more.

EXERCISE – Two heads?
Try writing with a friend. There are some very successful
writing partnerships around. If you're lucky you may find you
can bounce ideas off each other and you both improve your
writing skills. Try it for fun or try producing a best-seller.

I learned a lot from a writing partner, especially as he was
used to writing in the genre we tackled and generously passed
on his knowledge to me.

## The secret

There isn't one. Every time we write may be different. Even
established novelists may not use the same method every time.
Each book is different. Each method of writing one is different.
The same goes for short stories, articles, anything.

There is no right or wrong way of doing things. If you're told
that you should plan your book by writing an outline and you're
happy with that, go for it. If you fancy writing a sentence and
then seeing where it leads you then go for it. If you have the
closing sentence and then a bit of the middle, and you keep
hopping about until you've got the whole thing written, what's
the problem? Whatever works for you. And that whatever may
change each time you sit down to write.

## Rewards

Successes should be celebrated, however big or small. Writing
can be all about celebrations and rewards.

## 500 words

When writing longer pieces, or getting back into writing after a
break, reward yourself upon reaching 500 words. Get those
words down on paper or screen and then dip into a bag of giant
chocolate buttons. You may prefer an apple (really?) or a cup of
coffee.

## Half-way

Writing a book? A meal and a good bottle of wine will cheer you as you reach your half-way mark. The middle is the point at which so many writers give up so it makes sense to celebrate reaching it and will give you the impetus to attack the second half.

## Finish and celebrate again

You've typed The End. This is the time for the Biggie. Your Giant Reward. Plan a big celebration, be it a holiday with your loved ones, or a party to let everyone know you are back in circulation, for a while anyway.

Know what your reward is going to be. Think about it often and it will help you get to the final page of your work.

# 6

# When the going gets tough

## Stop procrastinating

Change 'I'll start it tomorrow/next week' to 'I've got five minutes now.'

## Bribery works

It can be difficult to motivate yourself into producing work, especially if no-one has commissioned it and you have no deadline. You don't want to sit and write but know you should, so how about bribing yourself?

'I'll do one page and then I can stop,' might work for you.

## Sweet treat

When the going gets tough, stop for chocolate. But make sure you carry on afterwards.

## Do some research

This especially applies when writing a novel.

There's very little point in sitting, looking at a screen. Your mind goes blank and the harder you try to come up with something the less likely it is to happen. It's the same as when you're trying to remember a name and it won't come to you. Do something else instead and, by switching your mind off the problem, hey presto! Like magic the name is there.

Leave the problematic writing and go out and do some research. You know what you need to find out, or you should have a list of the points you need to research. Take an afternoon off and visit the Museum, Library, or that person who may be able to help you. There's no guilt because you are still actually working but it's not work you can do at the keyboard.

## Write the dedication first

Let the book follow. This really helped when I was working on my first book. It was for pre-teens and about cycle racing. A lot of the information was based on personal experience so it made sense to dedicate the book to those young boys who had cycled, trained and raced alongside my son. And I wanted to include our dear friend, Duncan, who had died whilst out on his bike. The first words I wrote were – In memory of Duncan and the Lost Boys. The Lost Boys being the schoolboys who had grown up, many of whom had left the sport.

This dedication helped when the going got tough. I would turn back to those words and they gave me the confidence to carry on.

Write your dedication – to your husband, children, parents, lover, whoever, and look back at it whenever the going gets tough for you.

## Today is …

… a blank canvas. Pencil in some writing time. Don't worry if it doesn't happen. Whatever happens today may be fodder for tomorrow's writing.

## Today is …

… a blank canvas. Don't pencil in any writing time. INK it in. Don't break that date. Go steady with your writing. Love it so much that you want to spend time with it every day. Make it a lasting and productive relationship.

## Today is …

… another step on your writing path. It could be a large stride or a tiny, uncertain wobble. But it is another step and you will get there in the end.

## Today is ...

... the day you start that novel.

## Today is ...

... the day you stop procrastinating and get on with your dream. Remember a dream stays a dream until you do something about it.

## Today is ...

... the day you act on your dream.

## Today is ...

... when you start focusing on what you have done and not what you haven't done.

## Eating an elephant

You eat an elephant one bite at a time. Every thousand mile march has a first step. These are only two wise sayings. There are many more that all tell us the same thing. We all need to start somewhere and even a little start is a start. If you never start you can never finish so get that first line written. Then add another.

## Baby steps ...

Sometimes you may get panicky. The workload is too much. Your dreams are too many. There is not enough time. It is then that I repeat 'Baby steps'.

I once saw a post on a social networking site. A writer had an idea that had grown so large he thought it would make four novels, not the one he'd imagined. It was too big for him. He was floundering and had resorted to asking online strangers for advice. The responses were all different. I would have been even more confused by the time I'd read through them. He needed to do this alone. How? By taking Baby Steps, that's how.

## Love and glue

Those are the words Glynis Scrivens used at the end of her email to me. Love is normal. But what's all this about glue?

I'd been complaining about some work in progress. Actually, it wasn't progressing but needed completing before I could move on to anything else. 'You need to stick your bum to that seat,' said my friend and that's why she sent me love and *glue*.

Are you struggling with a piece of work? Please accept this *glue*.

## Be gripped by your storyline

If you aren't why should anyone else be? It's happened to me. I've been working on a short story and it hasn't inspired me. Sometimes you need to leave it alone until that new idea arrives that will enable you to give your work in progress sparkle. In the meantime, don't get bored.

Get up and dance. (There's no-one watching.)

## The Yeti, Fairies, Time-warps, Writers' Block

Do any of the above exist? Maybe. It depends who you are and what you want to believe. Personally, I'd love to see a yeti, I hope there are fairies at the bottom of the garden and I know someone who has been through a time-warp. (Hi A.L.)

As for writers' block, I know some writers who believe in it and others who don't.

I wasn't allowed a block when I was working for a newspaper. The editor would have laughed if I'd told him work was impossible that day. Other writers struggle with it.

My advice – go for the *It's only another myth* theory.

## Writers' block or writers' rest?

You think you're suffering from a block? Don't panic. Consider it part of the writing process.

Novelist Eileen Ramsay put it this way. 'The fields outside my house look very bare and barren at the moment. Nothing is going on. Don't believe it. An unbelievable amount of activity is going on underground. It will take several months but boy, come and look out of the window in March.'

'That's what writing is like. Accept the fallow moments. Do other things. Your fingers may not be working but your head and heart are.'

## Staying alive

If you've ever bragged about doing a twelve-hour stint at the keyboard, don't get too smug. Take care. Substituting writing for living will, eventually, make you stale. Live and write.

## Don't turn to Solitaire, Facebook, emails ...

Many years ago I asked a friend, 'What are you working on?'

'Nothing. I'm playing Spider Solitaire,' was her reply.

The plot of her novel was giving her problems so she'd switched on to the Games on her computer. Games don't solve anything.

At that time I had a boss who played computer Patience all day, every day. Instead of sending out invoices and looking for more contracts he flicked cards until his eyeballs ached and his eyelids became swollen.

Computers can make writing easier. We can cut and paste, move whole scenes from Friday to Tuesday with the click of a few keys. Thousands of words can be deleted, changed, spell- and grammar-checked, printed out time and time again. Wonderful. But way back then I wondered how much more could be achieved if there had been no games on computers?

I would often make myself a cup of tea, and click on to a game of Solitaire instead of tackling a difficult scene in a story. Why? Can anyone think of a more boring game? Did it do me any good? No, it made my eyes sore and it certainly didn't increase my word count.

One day I bit the bullet and deleted the Games section from my computer.

But now there are even more distractions. Emails. Facebook. Twitter and other time-consuming stuff yet to be invented. Of course these things are useful and sometimes interesting, but they can so easily eat up an hour, an afternoon or an evening. Ration the time spent on them and don't turn to them in times of a writing crisis. Aim to keep on writing until the problem is solved. Then you can tell all your friends on Facebook.

## Hup, two, three

Physical exercise can help if your mind seizes up – even running on the spot for five minutes. Get up now and try it. Hup, two, three.

Go for a walk. That's a double whammy – fresh air and exercise.

Make like a cat and stretch, stretch, stretch.

Run up and down the stairs a few times.

Do anything active. It'll get the circulation going and stimulate those little grey cells.

## Down, two, three

Total relaxation can help if your mind seizes up – chill out in a comfy chair for ten minutes. Stop and do some deep breathing. Lie down with your arms at your sides and relax. If you can manage it, meditate. Try to empty your head of all thoughts or, and this is slightly easier, let them go as they arrive.

If you fall asleep, don't worry. You fell asleep because you needed a rest. You'll work more easily now.

## Record your dreams

If you do fall asleep during the previous tip then, when you wake, do write down any dreams you've had. Dreams can be interesting, revealing our hopes and fears. Buy a dream book so that you can decipher your dreams if their meanings aren't apparent.

A tiny dream-piece might prove useful in your writing.

Don't beat yourself up about day-dreaming. You're not wasting time. Day-dreams can be really helpful but, like night-time dreams, they fade very quickly so capture them in a notebook, on a piece of paper, on screen. Do this before they dissolve into the busy day.

Back in Junior school, Miss Tipper, a kind, thoughtful and insightful teacher, allowed me some day-dreaming time each day. 'Day-dreamers go far in life,' she said. And I believe her.

EXERCISE – Magic moments
Sometimes I doubt my abilities. That's the time for a Magic Moment. It works for me so I'll pass on instructions for coming up with your own, in case you ever feel like giving up.

A Magic Moment is something to relive. It will lift you, make you smile, and put things into perspective.

I use my Dog's Dinner moment. Let me explain. Dog's Dinner is a children's story of mine that was accepted for an anthology. When my copy of this book arrived my name was on the contents page, right in the middle of all the authors I worship – Anne Fine, Roger McGough, Penelope Lively, Michael Rosen ... In fact my name was the only one I didn't recognise. Never in my wildest dreams had I envisaged being in such illustrious company. This was definitely a Magic Moment.

Now you need one of your own. What is your best writing moment? It could be your first sale, or when you met someone – a favourite author perhaps, or when you found a lovely new writing friend, or your group praised your work. It should be a writing related moment that you can bring to the surface when times are hard – one that will make you smile and lift those spirits. Hopefully you'll have more than one to call upon.

# 7

# Sound advice

## Because I'm worth it

Always send work to the highest paying market first. This may sound like stating the obvious but many writers don't do this. In the distant past, I was delighted when one of my stories was accepted so immediately sent another to the same market. It was turned down so I gave myself a good talking to and then sent it to a market that I knew paid more but which I had thought was too broad-based for my efforts. Wrong attitude, but I was newly born as a writer back then and frightened to send work to Big People. The better paid market accepted my offering and asked for more. They also sent me a cheque for four times the amount the lower market had paid me.

New writers, you are huge. You can achieve whatever you want. Forget little egos. Stand up straight. Stretch. Smile. You're big enough to be seen in the best places. Go for it and tell yourself you're worth it.

## That'll do

Have you ever said that about a piece of work? Perhaps it was at the end of a long writing session, when you were tired or hungry, or it was time to go off to work or pick up the kids from school.

You've been working on a story, a chapter, an article and you think you are almost there. It's looking good, sounding good but there's something missing – something you can't quite fathom. This is not the time to say, 'It'll do.'

You can be sure it won't do. It won't do at all. You are in the wrong frame of mind to be making important decisions.

It's time to press SAVE and return another time, another day, after supper or the following morning. Save it for when you are fresh again and can look at it with wide eyes.

And remember this. There's a great difference between 'That'll do,' and 'That'll do nicely.'

## It gets better

A friend is reading your novel for you. They yawn over the first chapter and you say, 'It gets better.' It's no good having a wonderful article or brilliantly plotted story if your best work isn't at the beginning. Correction. If your best work isn't all the way through.

I struggled with a choice from book club. 'It gets better,' one member told me. 'You need to persevere.' But I shouldn't have to and neither should anyone else. An editor or publisher's reader won't.

## Aim for perfection

Keep aiming for perfection. Never believe you have achieved it.

You have to aim to be as good as you can possibly be and this means checking every sentence, every phrase, every word, every comma and fullstop.

Have you ever met anyone who has considered they have achieved perfection? There are a few around and arrogant is the word that springs to mind.

Perfection is something you aim for, not brag about.

## Can't do dialogue?

If you find writing dialogue difficult, don't ignore the problem. Tackle it. The same goes for plot, characterisation, grammar, punctuation …

Work on your weaknesses.

## Leaking energy

Never talk about an on-going project. Talking about it takes energy from it and makes it stale.

## Money, money, money

Write for love but think of the money. Writers deserve to be paid exactly the same as any other profession. Make sure you have a professional attitude when it comes to being paid but remember to value your work more than the money you get for it.

## Deep breaths and relax

The faster I type, the higher my shoulders lift. That's not good.

If you nodded when you read that then you, like me, need to train yourself to relax at the keyboard.

Check your chair, your position at the desk, the height of your screen. Get comfortable.

In the meantime check in for an Indian head, neck and shoulder massage. Bliss!

## Tottering piles

A friend has been involved in the sport of cycling for his entire life. In his loft are copies of a weekly cycling magazine. He has every single issue since 1950.

I've received every issue of one particular writing magazine, ever since it began, but as a new issue arrives an old one is recycled or passed to a friend. Out-dated news and information is no use.

If you are seriously interested in writing, in learning the business side of it, in keeping up with current trends, reading of others' successes, being inspired and educated, then you should be subscribing to a writing magazine. Or several. Because you can never know it all and one good tip, or market, per issue is enough.

**EXERCISE – Throwing out**
**Go and throw away your old Writers' and Artists' Yearbook or Writers' Handbook. Buy a new one. You wouldn't keep a five-year-old bus timetable. It would hold out of date information.**

Sort out that heap of old magazines. You need to read current ones to see what editors want. It's no good poring over a year-old magazine. That will only tell you what was needed twelve months ago. You need to write for tomorrow's market by studying today's magazines.

## You what!!!!

An excess of exclamation marks shows a true beginner. That's what a kind editor told me when he returned my very first offering. Immediately I checked my work and boy, was he right. There was an ! at the end of almost every piece of dialogue. There was an ! whenever I wanted to make a point of how witty I was being. The number of exclamation marks that had been crammed into that first story must have been record breaking.

Save exclamation marks for real exclamations such as Ouch! Help! Look out!

Leave them off the end of long sentences as they are not necessary.

Now rush off to do an ! count!

## Soapy stuff

I have often heard writers knocking soaps. Why? Someone's earning good money writing them. Think of the skill needed. There are all those plots to come up with. All that characterisation. Not to mention the huge audience they attract.

Now transfer those thoughts to your novel or work in progress. Wouldn't you like to earn some money from your writing? And how about plots and characters? Do they come easily to you? How about having a huge audience waiting in anticipation for your work?

Writers can learn a lot from watching a soap or two. Don't knock them until you've tried them.

Actually that can be said for most things.

EXERCISE – Soap in your eyes
Watch your favourite soap (or watch one for the first time). Keep a notebook and pen in your lap and note down how many scenes there are in one episode. More than you think. When it's finished see if you can write a few scenes to continue the plot threads that were covered. It's good writing practice and you may become a convert. Did you ask 'converted to what?' You may get hooked and become a soap addict or you may want to become a writer of a soap.

If so, enjoy the money!

## It may be taken down

When friends visit they often bring snippets of information and gossip that I later find myself using as story plots. To save any fallings out I greet visitors with a warning. 'You do not have to say anything, but anything you do say may be taken down and used in a story later.'

If your friends are about to bare their souls they need to know that you aren't brilliant at keeping secrets and may well sell them, in a disguised version. Some will be happy with that fictionalised version. Others will not. If you want to keep your friends, give them a warning as they cross your threshold.

## An apple for the teacher

Signed up for a correspondence course? Many of us have, especially at the beginning of our writing lives. Some ended up as real writers by the end of their course. Some became tutors because they enjoyed the course, had learned from it and knew they wanted to pass that knowledge on to others.

These online or distance courses cost money and you'd be amazed at how many would-be-students cough up the cash yet never complete the course. Don't do that. Set yourself deadlines and stick to them. If there are areas you are not interested in think yourself into newspaper reporter mode. Reporters write what has to be written. They don't say, 'I don't fancy that. I don't want to do it.' Bite the bullet and get on with it, or contact your tutor and explain why you can't do it. These blips shouldn't prevent you from finishing the course.

Always finish the course.

## Is that me?

It's not a good idea to tell a friend or family member that you've put them into your story or book. For starters they might ask for a percentage of the profits. On the other hand they may not like your portrayal of them. What you see in them is not necessarily what they see in themselves.

## Proof of the above

My Aunt's new stair-lift gave me an idea for a story. The editor of my chosen market rather liked grumpy old ladies so I had to turn my Auntie into a suitable old misery-guts. I didn't know that she took that magazine on a regular basis as she loved the puzzles. Of course, when she saw my name she read the story and she didn't speak to me for weeks afterwards.

My mother, who was used to being the subject of many short stories, explained to her that this grumpy old bat wasn't how I saw her. It was all made-up. I'd got the idea from her stair-lift and had to make a story around it.

I didn't get a Christmas card that year.

## EXERCISE – Use revenge

**Lower your blood pressure by using revenge. If someone's annoyed you give them acne. Bump them off. Change their sex. Turn that awful receptionist at the doctor's into a man – give her whiskers (don't bother if she's already got them).**

## A bad day?

Have you ever told yourself you've not written a decent word all day?

If that time ever arrives check through your work again. Somewhere there will be a decent sentence, a phrase, a description ...

Everyone has bad days. Everyone has good days. Learn to roll with them. Tell yourself, tomorrow will be good. Tomorrow I will write as if I am a genius. I will be totally inspired, on fire.

And if you are still saying you didn't write a decent word then you must be one harsh critic. Be gentler with yourself.

## A boring life

Some people will tell you that 'not a lot' has happened to them, They've had a boring life. The truth is that what is a normal everyday occurrence to them can often seem boring. If a man had spent fifty years hand-weaving carpets then he might think no-one else would be interested in what he did for a living. Wrong! I wouldn't know where to begin, or end, and the middle would be a mystery to me too.

One elderly lady's 'nothing much' turned out to be surviving divorce when it was considered shocking, bringing up five children on her own, working at three jobs because she was too proud to take 'charity' (social security), working in Munitions during the War ...

All these situations were new and interesting to me, normal and boring to the octogenarian. She had enough material to write a family saga.

'No-one would want to read about me,' she said at a writers' workshop. (If only so-called celebrities had this attitude.)

I explained that she could write her life story as it really happened so that her grand-children and great-grandchildren could learn about her experiences. Or she could use parts of her life, mixing them with fiction. She could even take events and use them as a basis for short stories.

Many writers forget that what is an everyday occurrence to

them is a rarity to someone else.

## Etiquette

Etiquette. (Accepted standards of proper social or professional behaviour.) This is a quaint word worth remembering when approaching a well-known writer. Never thrust a half-finished manuscript under their nose and ask them to read it for you. Don't thrust a completed one either. You can ask if they'd be willing to read your work and how much they will charge. All writers need to make a living and their time is valuable.

## Don't hog your hero

Naturally you are elated to have met and actually be chatting to your favourite author but don't monopolise their time. Others will want to speak to them too.

## A scary experience

It doesn't matter how you do it, just get it done. I didn't and when my computer suddenly died I lost work.

Make sure you do it. Regularly. A memory stick, CD, hard copy or one of the online programmes that save work for you. New methods are always turning up.

## Why wait?

When I was a new writer I'd send out a story then sit and wait until its fate was decided. I waited for the postman day after day and I didn't care what the news was. Any news would be welcome, whether it be a 'yes please' or 'no thanks'.

Once I knew the fate of my work I could start a new story. I did this waiting lark for a couple of years until I met Irene Yates, someone further along the writing path than I was. She advised me to aim for three pieces of work out at any one time. Once that number was achieved she said I should aim higher. Try for five or ten or ...

I reached thirty-nine. It became my record to beat. Now I know of other writers who have achieved double that figure but I wasn't competing with them. The only competition I had was with myself. My work output grew and grew, and stressing about whether something was going to be accepted or rejected became a thing of the past. Because there was so much out there doing the rounds, there was always something due to be returned or accepted.

The 'write and wait' system seems to be fairly prevalent amongst new writers. Do yourself a favour. Give it up now.

## Had your first novel accepted?

Fantastic! You know what you've achieved and the effort that's gone into it. Many people will be proud of you. I will. Be proud of yourself too but remember this – you shouldn't automatically expect your kids to be impressed.

## Read your final draft out loud

Mistakes and repetition will leap out at you, if there are any. Read to yourself, the cat, the wall ... And make sure you always test dialogue by reading it aloud.

## Writing a stage play?

Read your script walking around the room as the actors eventually will, walking around a stage.

## Want an agent?

Write to half a dozen every six months, then one day, maybe ... In the meantime build up a writing CV by selling short pieces to magazines and newspapers.

## Writing yourself into

Many writers write themselves into a piece of work. It's a sort of warming up exercise, getting to know your characters and plot, discovering where you are going and what exactly you are writing. It's okay to do this but once you're done go back and cross out your first paragraph and then the next one until you reach the real beginning of your story.

## Do not approach

If you ever see someone reading your book on a bus, train or in the park, resist telling them you wrote it. They won't believe you and you might scare them. The public don't expect writers to be wandering around.

## Spare parts

Always keep spare parts handy – ink jets, cartridges, paper. It's part of being professional.

## Never iron when you can write

Writing has to be the important task. You can use mundane tasks as thinking time. I actually enjoy ironing, in silence and on my own. Many writing problems have been solved and new ideas hatched at the ironing board.

## Don't hurt kittens

An editor once received hundreds of complaints about a twist at the end of a story she'd published. There'd never been a complaint about any of the hundreds of stories involving wives murdering their husbands or lovers.

Take care over who is murdered or abused in your stories. Never hurt kittens!

# 8

# Learning from others

## Getting out

Always go to talks by successful writers when they visit your area. If you pick up one new tip it will be worth it. Go to at least one conference or workshop every year. I know of many writers who began by attending conferences and ended up by teaching at them.

Remember that writer who has just given a forty-five minute talk and held you spellbound may actually be nervous, or shy. Not all writers are social butterflies. Many don't like the part of the business when they have to get out there and sell themselves as well as their books. You won't know if you're one of them until you're in the same position.

Aim for it.

## Light bulb moments

When I was attempting a novel, after writing hundreds of short stories, a writing friend suggested slowing the pace and to 'add frocks and food'. It was a light bulb moment.

The historical novelist and saga writer, Freda Lightfoot, mentioned in a class that old newspapers were helpful when writing historical fiction. I had some that were over one hundred years old so immediately decided to transfer something I was thinking of writing back to that era. Another light bulb moment.

Novelist Julie Cohen once told an audience how she struggled to change the length of her work. She had been used to writing for Mills and Boon but had a contract for some stand-alone books which were far longer than she was used to writing. She tried adding more sub-plots and extra characters and had then been given some excellent advice which helped her and proved to be another light bulb moment for me. What had she been told? 'Don't add more. Go deeper.'

Be sure to save your light bulb moments in a notebook – before they go out.

## Never give up on loved ones

Short story writer Glynis Scrivens says, 'A story I wrote four years ago was sent everywhere and rejected by everyone. But I still believed in it. So, I *rested* it for a couple of years and then sent it out again and it was accepted. Twice!'

This goes to prove that writers should never throw anything out. Re-read the work you produced several years ago and if it sounds good then test it on those markets again. You may need to tweak it or do a complete rewrite, or maybe you can't believe how good it sounds when you take another look after that resting period.

When my daughter was twelve she went on a field trip with her school. It was an experience for both of us as she replaced the thermal undies I had packed with sparkly nail polish and comic books. This was all written up as a short story but it didn't sell even though it did the rounds of all the women's magazines. A couple of years later, after *resting*, I tried it again. No luck. But I still believed in this story so kept sending it out every few years and finally, thirty years later it sold!

When do you finally give up on a piece? No-one can tell you that. As Glynis says, 'In the end it's gut instinct, isn't it?'

## There is no beginning too small

A bookmark is stuck to the noticeboard above my computer. It bears simple words of wisdom – *There is no beginning too small*. That's something we should all remember.

How many times have you had a good idea but not known where to begin? Perhaps it was a novel. Perhaps something much shorter. Time is short so it will have to be written in little pieces, ten minutes or 100 words at a time. There is no beginning too small. I've proved it by writing an opening line for a short story and then getting stuck. Fifteen words do not a story make, but later I went back to this piece and added another paragraph, and another. Finally it was complete.

A small beginning is better than no beginning at all. There's also no rule to say that your small beginning can't be your end, or your middle. It can be any part of your story, book or article.

When I was at one of Jane Wenham Jones's workshops she told the class to shut out everything and write for five minutes – and we did. Most of us completed at least half a page, many a whole page in that short time. 'Imagine doing it another six times,' we were told. Imagine. You'd end up with far more than a small beginning.

It's another twist on the write fifty words idea. Once you start writing and get into it you can lose yourself and the writing flows. It's the getting going that can be the hardest part. We can sit and stare at the blank page or screen for hours waiting for inspiration or, in my case, stare at the wall with the bookmark on it, read the words and get on with something, however small.

**EXERCISE – Take five**
**Shut out everything and write for five minutes now.**

## Knocking on doors

If at first you don't succeed, try, try and try again. Apparently that worked out well for Robert the Bruce (or was that his spider?) but what about writers?

We have all heard about successful novelists who went through countless rejections before someone intelligent enough to see their genius signed them up. You might be one to go down this route, or you might be the writer who never gets a novel published. If you've tried and tried, in your chosen field, and still failed when do you stop banging your head on that door that never opens?

Let's say a day dawns when you realise that you are spending your life churning out words that no-one wants to read. What then? You step off that road and take a side turning. Why? Because if you're not cut out to be a novelist then perhaps you can be a great short story writer or sell hundreds of articles or write a shelf-full of non-fiction books.

I'd like to tell you about my lovely friend, John Newton. He wrote several novels but, and he admitted this to me, they were flat. Something was missing. Eventually John tried something else. Humour. He used a lot of personal experience in his articles, writing laugh-out-loud pieces about life as a father and grand-father and what his life was like being a grumpy old man. He sold the first few to a magazine and they proved so popular that the editor asked him to write a regular column for them. His work delighted readers and the members of his writing group.

Maybe it's time for you to change tack and step out of your comfort zone.

There are lots of doorways into the world of writing. If your first choice appears locked then try another.

## Understanding the ice splinter

Is it ethical to people watch, and write about those characters, when collected from a dramatic situation? Of course it is. And lots of writers do.

I was alone, driving along narrow twisting lanes over the top of a mountain. It was 2 am. There was no light in sight and added to the darkness was a thick mist. This is a perfect setting for a spine-chiller, I thought and then cursed myself for being heartless. I was driving to the hospital where my husband was sick, really sick, and all I could think about was a setting for a story.

Later, as he was recovering, I made notes about the other patients and their visitors and ended up with several pages of thoughts, feelings, characters, bits of dialogue ...

I hated myself for being able to do that – to think about writing at such a time. Then Janie Jackson asked, 'Remember *The Snow Queen*? The little boy, Kay, had a splinter of ice in his heart. Writers can be like that. There's a part of us that can stand to one side and do the observing bit, even while dreadful or emotional events are taking place.'

Graham Greene is said to have come up with the term – the splinter of ice in a writer's heart.

It's not the best bit of being a writer but at least now I'm accepting it, so don't feel guilty if you come across your own ice splinter.

## A mystery muscle

Short story writer, Elizabeth Moulder, told me, 'I will never ever let my writing muscle get flabby again. It's so hard to get back.' She'd not written for a month and once back at her desk found herself staring at a blank screen.

Is there a writing muscle? Not in any anatomy books. But it exists. Trust me (and Betty).

The expression *use it or lose it* is true. Your writing muscle won't be gone for ever but allow it to turn to flab and you'll have a frustrating time getting it firm again. In order to tone up that mystery muscle you'll have to overcome the blank screen, write a lot of rubbish and keep on writing. It's far simpler to keep it toned with regular exercise.

## Using a diary

A few years ago, a friend who juggles consultancy work with crime-writing gave me some tips on time-management and persuaded me to keep a diary for work.

Apparently a diary should be bulky enough so that it has to be left at home then, if anyone asks if you can do something – have dinner, speak at a meeting – not having it to hand gives you the opportunity to say, 'I need to check my diary.' No need for hasty decisions which might be regretted later.

My well-organised friend says a diary will help you manage your writing time. If you had a full-time office job your day would be structured with certain tasks to complete, so all you need to do is apply the same reasoning to your writing.

This is the plan. Each morning you open your diary to check your projects for the week, which you will already have listed. They get crossed off as they are achieved. You write down successes, rejections and anything else writing related so that you can see at a glance how your time has been spent.

A diary kept solely for writing purposes sounds like a good idea and it may well work for you. Try it and see. (I'm not organised enough and gave up after a few months.)

## Have an alter-ego

Have you ever felt the presence of some disapproving person peering over your shoulder as you write? Perhaps it's your mother tutting loudly as you sweat over a sex scene, or a school teacher from long ago who didn't approve of your literary efforts. How do you get rid of them? You need an alter-ego.

An alter-ego is not simply another name, it's a whole new identity.

Writer and hypnotherapist, Steve Bowkett, uses his own name when writing for children but he wanted to write horror stories, complete with graphic gory details and found it difficult as he knew his mother would be offended.

'I had to come up with an alter-ego,' he said. 'He freed me to write in a previously untried style. As no-one knew him, no-one could disapprove.'

According to Steve, you should pick a name which has absolutely no connection to you. Don't trawl the family tree or choose a name with the same initials as yours. Your alter-ego should be a random choice. Try letting a book fall open, then select a first name from that page. Try another book and another page for a surname.

Using this method I became Steffi Dennis. Steffi is overflowing with confidence. She is taller than me, and slimmer, and she forced me to write a comic, sexy novel (as yet unpublished). You have been warned.

## In the zone

Have you ever had a time when a piece of writing almost wrote itself? This is because you had lost yourself in it, travelled from your conscious state to your creative one and become totally immersed in your work. It's wonderful when that happens.

This is when we are in our element, in the zone. You forget you're at the keyboard or sitting with pen in hand because you're in the story, article, novel or poem. It's a magical transformation from writing to living the words.

How do you get into the zone? It's not something you can consciously do. If you think about it then the magic won't happen. It occurs when you are so deeply engrossed in your work that you become part of it.

Novelist Kate Lord Brown calls it the flow. She says, 'Flow is like catching a perfect wave – when your writing is going so well it is effortless. You are present but somewhere else entirely and can lose hours at a time given the chance. I write very visually, and I *see* the story. When the work is flowing easily, it's almost like transcribing a mental film.'

'Sometimes you glimpse this effortless absorption in children's faces – I wonder if they slip more easily into the zone than we do? Perhaps as you get older there are so many things running through your mind it becomes less easy to slow down and let go.'

Perhaps a way into this is by clearing your mind and remaining young? Whatever it is, enjoy it while you're there.

## Do as I say, not as I do

The truth of that dawned on me when I noticed a comment on Simon Whaley's blog about writing workshops.

Simon recalled the tutor telling the class to go through magazines a page at a time asking themselves, 'Could I write for this page ... or this one?'

Isn't that a good idea? Now for the confession. I was that tutor but I'd never actually done that. I'd only ever thought I would, one day. Later I tried it out.

I've always known about the opportunities in the women's weekly 'tabloid' style of magazines – letters, tips, operations, complaints about men. (I never consider the latter.) Monthly magazines had openings too. I could write about holidays, places I'd visited. Right away I turned out a letter responding to something on the letters page of one of them.

I've always thought that if I could pick up one new tip from another writer then visiting his/her class has been worthwhile. This time I picked up a tip from my own class, from my own mouth! It brings a whole new meaning to *Do as I say, and not as I do*.

## Get cracking

Got a contract, a commission, an idea? Get cracking. Life and challenges tend to leap out when you least expect them.

Your computer chuckles to itself when you've not backed up your work and decides to teach you a lesson by crashing. Your memory stick has amnesia. Pleading the excuse of computer problems isn't exactly original. It's down there with 'the cheque's in the post'.

If the family are due a crisis then it is inevitably when you're halfway through a book.

Give yourself all the time you can and get cracking.

This is a case of 'do as I say and not as I do' as, once again, I'm in the same predicament. I was given a deadline for this book and faffed about until an email arrived saying, 'Your book is conspicuous by its absence.' That message was also a good kick up the proverbial.

### EXERCISE – Plan for success
Visualise what success will mean to you, how you will celebrate it, what changes it will make to the way you live and think.

On a course she ran on motivation for writers, Solange Hando told the class that their homework was to have their photo taken. They needed to put on a big smile, hold up their thumbs and shout, 'I am a writer' as the camera clicked. Some went a little further than that and shouted, 'I am a best-selling writer.'

Try this for yourself. Get someone to take your picture. Pin it up near your desk where you can see it constantly and remind yourself that you can do it. Don't allow the tiniest doubt to creep in. Why bother with doubts when you can plan for success?

9

# Boomerangs (rejections)

## Kicking the cat

'Be quietly confident. Realise that a returned manuscript is part of your apprenticeship.' Those are my own words, written and offered to other writers. Why did I write them? Does quietly confident describe me when yet another story is returned?

It certainly didn't when I began sending my work out. In those days I gave into my natural reactions. I swore and sulked. I mastered ranting and raving back then.

Better out than in, as my Granny used to say.

Thankfully, as my apprenticeship progressed so my reactions toned down. There were fewer tears, fewer expletives. Eventually the stage was reached when I could philosophically dump the rejected work on my desk and refrain from even peeping at it until I was calm and quietly confident that I could do so without swearing.

Wasting all that energy was pretty pointless. Don't do it.

## Why settle for quietly confident?

Maybe it's okay to be quietly confident about your creation. But how about going that one stage further? Or several stages? Should you be quietly confident when you've worked hard and know your work is as good as you can ever make it? Maybe.

There's nothing wrong with being reserved but, what the hell, you're on your own, there's no-one to see you so how about a quick dance around and a loud Wahey! Wooey! Zippedee-doo-dah!

## Do I need to say this?

If at first you get a rejection, try, try and try again. I've heard of someone who didn't believe in giving up and sold their 99th story.

## Don't save rejection letters

What use is that? How many times have you heard of, or read about, writers who save their rejection letters? I've heard some say they have enough to wallpaper a room.

However fancy the letter headings may be, decorating the bathroom with them is not a good idea. Relaxing in the tub would be impossible when surrounded by all that negativity.

Read them and, if they are standard 'no thank-yous', drop them in the recycling.

## What to take note of

If yours is not the normal printed rejection but, instead, has something personal in it, then do take note. Please.

When I started out I believed a no meant no. I didn't take any notice of the personal comments those rejection letters contained. Years later I realised that any lines of encouragement from editors, who had taken some precious moments to add them, were genuinely meant.

Don't disregard anything that may have been scrawled across the bottom telling you that the editor would be happy to read more of your work. They do mean it.

## What to keep

Go for the positive attitude and keep a folder for acceptances instead. And if you want to be really positive add photocopies of cheques received for your work or, as is so often the case now, the bank remittance advice notes.

## Superstitions

Kissing submissions, crossing fingers, touching wood ... whatever works for you.

## Only believe the good superstitions.

Here's a not so good one. If the letters X, Y and Z are all used in the final sentence of a book it will be the last the writer ever pens. Don't let that concern you. What are the odds?

## Rejection superstition

I use scrap paper to print out first drafts of stories, articles or chapters from a novel. What I never do, as I am superstitious about it, is to use the backs of rejection letters. Bad karma, don't you think?

## 24-hour rule

Once recovered from a rejection it was time for me to go back to it and see what was wrong. Sometimes it was nothing. Sometimes there was a major flaw. Sometimes they were never revisited – until I discovered the 24-hour rule. This is when a rejected piece of work is only allowed to sit on your desk for a maximum of one day – 24 hours – before being sent off to another market.

Naturally, if it's a novel or any long piece of writing then a longer time is needed. Don't let it sit there until eventually it's pushed into a drawer and given up on. Give yourself a time limit. A week, maybe a fortnight, but as long as you believe in it keep sending it out and one day you'll get a yes.

## Sorting the wheat

If you're lucky enough to get some feedback along with your rejection, what do you do? You act on it if it's a short story. But what about feedback on novels? I had a dozen different, and lovely, letters saying no to mine. Each one made a point about the book that the particular editor hadn't liked. One thought the main character wasn't feisty enough. Another thought she was too feisty. Someone didn't like the little sci-fi interludes (there weren't many), yet another said they made her laugh out loud.

Someone suggested using more viewpoints, someone else recommended fewer.

So, what do you do if you have half a dozen or more comments or critiques from editors?

If everyone makes the same comment then you have a problem and can fix it. If everyone says something different then that comes down to personal preferences and you can ignore them.

You can't please everyone. And that's the truth.

# 10

# Pen to paper

## Coming to life

We all know they are not really flesh and blood but we have to convince readers that our characters are exactly that. We have to imagine them so powerfully that they speak to us directly and in their own voices.

Don't put too tight a control on your imaginary friends. Allow them to express themselves and tell you their feelings and their own story. Eventually you will learn to live comfortably alongside them, know when to rein them in and when to allow them total freedom. By that time you will know your characters as well as you know your kids, friends and family.

EXERCISE

I'm not suggesting gory murder but how about chopping up a few friends? This exercise can produce some interesting results.

No axe needed.

Simply think of three people (same sex) and chop them each into three pieces. Write a sentence on the dress sense of each. Then another sentence on the physical attributes (excluding clothes, you've already done that). Now pen a final sentence on one thing that makes that friend special – a loud laugh, a great singing voice, a talent for making fairy cakes.

Now make three new people out of the three real ones.

Try it now.

## Apple cheeks

Avoid stereotypes. Everyone is unique. I've never seen an apple-cheeked old grandma with a shawl and twinkling eyes. Have you?

## An awkward gait

Did he shuffle, stumble, stagger or lurch? Did she limp, hobble, shamble? Each word means something slightly different. Please don't tell your reader the man had an awkward gait. Describe it to them. Let them see if he is shuffling or lurching.

When you see someone who moves in a certain way, like the lady in the long dress who floated, or the little boy who bounced as if he was on springs, make a note of exactly how they moved. Keep the description until you need it. Agatha Christie's Poirot moves in such a way that there is no mistaking him. Those little mincing steps are an essential part of the character.

## An interesting trait

'Really?' he'd say after every remark we made to him. It was an interesting, if annoying, trait.

She always placed a finger across her mouth and bit lightly upon it when she was deep in thought. Another interesting trait.

We all have them but it's usually others who notice. Start noticing these little peculiarities that people have. They are useful when you want to make your main character a real, alive-on-the-page person. They are useful to use as tags. A tag is when you insert one tiny thing so that it clicks with the reader. For example, Amy could chew her hair. Bob could run his fingers over his tattoo, Mrs Bell could squint. The reader would remember that one trait/tag and picture that character.

**EXERCISE**
**Try writing down no more than six words to describe a friend. My friend said, 'red hair and dimples' when asked how she would describe me. Isn't she lovely?**

**EXERCISE**
**Go to the supermarket and come back with a character. Or sit in town or the park and find one. For example, a giant of a young**

man with a trolley load of junk food was in front of me in the queue. I took him home, exactly as seen, and used him in a story.

## Clothes maketh

What sort of clothes do you wear? Jeans and T-shirt? Suit and tie? Flowery ethnic skirts with open-toed sandals? Do you immediately think business man when you hear suit? Do bandana and beads mean hippie?

Take a peep into your characters' wardrobes. Know what they look good in and know what they feel comfortable wearing. But beware! Not all suits are worn by business men. What about the homeless person who has been given a suit by some well-meaning charity? What about the vegetarian in an elegant gown? Why do so many people think vegetarians wear ethnic/hippie clothing? (I am one and I don't.)

When you dress your characters make sure you do not stereotype them. Allow them a few little quirks. The young bride in the white dress hiding the Doc Marten boots is just as real as the one whose satin shoes match the rest of the outfit.

## Blue sky thinking

A sky can be sunny, stormy, moody, grey, blue. We can simply say the sky was blue or we can study a blue sky and come up with a decent description.

**EXERCISE – Blue skies**
Take five and stare at the heavens. What does that sky really look like? Write a picture of it in your notebook and save it until you need a (blue, stormy, grey, moody) sky. And while you're checking out the sky take a good look at a few other things too. Trees, flowers, the scenery. Learn to look and make notes as you go along. You never know when they'll come in handy.

## Dialogitis

Beware! When you begin to edit friends' conversation as they are talking – seeing the words, and shortening their sentences – you have contracted dialogitis. Actually, it's a good affliction for writers.

## Comfy research

You don't need a computer. You don't need a library. All you have to do is put your feet up, have a cup of coffee to hand along with pen and paper, then switch on the television. Whatever you watch, be it soap, drama, documentary or one of those real-life docu-soaps you will get ideas for plots, characters or articles. Read the cast lists and write down any names that appeal. Take notes about those foreign settings and place names. Sip your coffee, relax and work, all at the same time.

## Am I in it?

Writers often worry that the friends and family members they use in stories will recognise themselves. I've discovered there are two types of reader. Those of the first type look for themselves in the books/stories, wanting to be included. Those of the second type are in there but don't recognise themselves because the writer has used the side of them they don't want to see.

There was an occasion when my in-laws came to visit and I had left a story lying around. It was all about my father-in-law and his dangerous driving. He often had sheep running into his car, and when in town he complained of having to drive around pots of flowers in the middle of the road (a pedestrianised area to us).

I couldn't really snatch my masterpiece out of his hands so waited for the big row when he read about his own escapades. It didn't materialise. He laughed, told me he loved it and finished with, 'What an idiot that bloke was.'

## Upsetting your relatives

My mother enjoyed featuring in my stories as long as they were 'nice' ones. She knew that I used her situations as fiction as I had when she said she could do with getting married again just to get the wedding presents and I promptly came up with a story based on that idea. She knew the published version was 'made up'. She hadn't actually carried out the fake wedding plans, or pretended to be jilted once she'd received and used all the gifts.

Some relatives don't understand. Either you leave them out of your stories or you teach them how a writer works.

# 11

# Like minds

## Advertise

Everyone needs at least one writing friend. No-one else understands the work we do. Join a group. Start your own. Find writing friends. Look in your local newspaper or on the information board in the library for a writing group. If you have no luck then place an advertisement asking if there are writers in your area. It doesn't matter if that friend lives on the opposite side of the planet. Glynis Scrivens came to me via the internet.

We all need support, sound advice and encouragement.

## Writing friends

You will need others who understand the writing life – people who will support you, be there to encourage you and be happy to share celebrations when you have a success. Make friends with other writers who have positive attitudes.

What we can do without are writing friends who are negative. No-one needs a fellow writer spouting doom and gloom, telling you there's very little point in writing a short story when the markets are so few, or you won't get anywhere unless you know someone at the top to give you a helping hand.

Stick with positive writing friends and make sure you are positive for them when they need it.

Drop the complainers.

## Coffee and cake, coffee and notebooks

Writing is a lonely business. Our invented characters can keep us company for hours but eventually we all feel the need to go out into the real world and socialise. Now here's the good news. You can socialise and write at the same time, and I'm not talking writers' groups here.

Some writers work in cafés but that still means being alone. Why not meet up with two or three writer-friends for coffee and write together? It works like this.

First you choose the swankiest café in town – one of those with squashy sofas and waiters with tiny bottoms/waitresses with curves (whichever turns you on). Two or three of you arrive around the same time, nab the squashy seating arrangement and its accompanying table so you have space for drinks plus notebooks and pens. Order whatever you fancy on the menu and once it's arrived, you begin.

Take it in turns to challenge each other to write for five or ten minutes on a certain subject then take out notepads and pens and pretend you're famous authors as you scribble away, only stopping to sip your designer coffees.

In the summer sit outside and write about passers-by. When it's cold sit on the sofa in the window and write about the skyline, roofs and rats.

Waiters tend not to disturb you if you are writing. Normally they would have waited until you'd got a mouthful of chocolate éclair before asking if everything was all right.

Ten minutes writing will always produce a sentence, a character or a scene to transfer to some other work. Gossiping over a second cuppa can come afterwards.

Don't monopolise the tables if the place is busy. Get a take-away coffee and cake and sit in the park.

**EXERCISE – Write with friends**
**Make a date with one or two writing friends. Meet in a café, park, garden centre, and get writing.**

## It's who you know

Never say, 'It's all right for him/her. They've got contacts.' Join a writers' group. Go to conferences, festivals, workshops, talks.

Meet other writers. Make your own contacts.

I didn't know any writers or anyone involved in publishing when I first began writing. My first contact with like-minded people was at a Creative Writing class. From there I joined a Writers' Circle. The members all wrote but weren't exactly household names. We received information from all sorts of sources and shared it, hence my introduction to magazines about writing, my first visit to a talk by a 'proper' writer, and my very first conference.

I remember chatting to a lovely man there who turned out to be Deric Longden. Shame I didn't realise who he was at the time. At my next conference I approached the fiction editor of a woman's weekly magazine. We chatted and she was lovely.

A talk by a novelist at our library yielded another name to add to my name-dropping list.

It's easy enough to do. You go out and meet people, other writers, editors, agents. And before you know it, like me, you can name-drop with the best of them.

By meeting writers, publishers and agents, by going to conferences and talks, you will pick up not only names to drop, but facts and information to keep. And one of those writers might be the fairy godmother or genie of the lamp that intro-duces you to an agent or publisher, or gives you a few words of advice which will set you on your way.

## Who to trust

Trying out your work at a good writers' group where constructive feedback is given, could prove useful. Some groups praise anything so you may have to try out a few before you find one where members give out useful feedback. Being a member of a writing group doesn't automatically make you a good critic. One member of a group I belonged to rarely read out any work but she was the best and most honest and careful critic I have ever had. She knew how to pick up on the tiniest things to help improve your work and she knew how to do it in a positive and charming manner. I learned to trust her. Other members read at each meeting and were good at their craft but they weren't good critics. One was positively destructive in her criticism. (A gentle word in her ear helped resolve that problem.) Don't assume that because someone is a good writer, they are also a good critic. Learn who to trust in your writing group.

**EXERCISE – Swapping**
**Try swapping work at your writers' group so that members read other members' work aloud. See how many of you can guess which particular story or poem has been written by which writer.**

**This can prove a really interesting exercise. A good reader can make a bad story sound interesting, and vice versa.**

## Give and take

Learn to give constructive criticism. Comment on the good points of another member's work and then cover the points where it could be improved. Offer your suggestions. Don't simply tell them it's badly written. Tell them where and how it can be fixed.

Learn to take destructive criticism. Some members will dish it out. If someone becomes a problem have a word with the secretary and ask them to have a quiet word with the offender.

Take an active part in your group. Don't sit there waiting to read your work. Concentrate on the others' contributions too. Help the secretary or become the secretary/treasurer/web editor ... You'll discover there's always a 'core' membership. These are the enthusiasts. Join them.

## And now for something different

The idea of writing a novel can be daunting. Perhaps that's why several writers' groups I know of have attempted group novels.

Our group simply asked for volunteers and suggested they

produce a 'chunk'. How big a chunk was for them to decide. No deadlines, no pressure and no plans for publication. This exercise was purely for fun but, strangely enough, it proved more fruitful than we could ever have imagined.

As the latest instalment was read out at each meeting, more volunteers stepped forward. A couple of poets realised they enjoyed writing fiction. Two of the men had an on-going and enjoyable competition as to who could write the best erotica. Writers who had always worked with hard facts suddenly turned out humour and everyone managed a cliff-hanger. In fact there were so many cliff-hangers that the challenge to take up the threads eventually became too difficult and the project was abandoned.

The fact that this masterpiece is lost to humankind doesn't matter a jot. It gave us no end of laughs and made people stretch themselves and try something different. We learned to try to work in a different genre every once in a while, whether it be reading it or writing it. I'd recommend this to any group. Recommend it to yours.

12

# Set yourself on fire

## Set yourself on fire

Travel writer and inspirational speaker, Solange Hando, writes down inspirational quotes on cards. She suggests writers keep a collection of these. Make sure they are in the first person, hence Michael Flatley's words, 'Pain is constant, whether it be physical, emotional, spiritual' will end not with 'You have to fight ...' but with 'I will fight my way through it.'

Keep a different quote-card on your desk each week. I would have said, 'And read it often,' but Solange assured us that the card being there was enough. Somehow our amazing brains absorb the words and act on them.

Did someone just say 'Weird'? Don't knock it until you've tried it. I did and it works for me.

## Finding the matches

You don't have any inspirational quotes to hand? Put 'inspirational quotes' into your search engine and see what crops up. Then all you need to do is pick and choose.

I expect you'll discover Ralph Waldo Emmerson this way. 'Nothing great was ever achieved without enthusiasm' or 'Our greatest glory is not in never failing, but in rising up every time we fail.'

Many years ago an old friend of mine discovered one just when she needed it. She was afraid of what was happening in her life and was thinking of running away. She had reached the corner of her road when she looked up and saw a bill-board advertising a brand of beer. Guess what that brand was called?

Courage!

She turned around, went home and solved her problems.

## Bigger bonfires

A few sentences are perfect to keep by your side but how about keeping an inspirational book on your bedside table. It needn't be about writing. It could be a motivational one about the whole of life. Or the biography of a famous writer who overcame all obstacles on his path to glory. Or it could be purely about writing and be filled with tips on how to do it, how to cope with the pitfalls, how to celebrate the joys.

There is always something to learn. There's always something to be reminded about too.

## Visualise

Go to the shelf in the library or bookshop where your book would be if it was written and published. Visualise it on that shelf. Make a space for it.

Want to see your book in print. Really want.

Lie down in a darkened room and visualise your work in a magazine, your book in your hands. Smell the paper. See the print. Feel the joy. Do this for five minutes and keep practising. Thoughts become things. (see www.tut.com)

## Plan the celebration

Make a list of the people you will call when your work appears in print. (Fellow writers are the most understanding. They've been there, done that.)

## Smile

Smile as you sit down to write. A smile is magic. It will make you feel happy and positive and that's a good way to begin anything.

**COMPASS
BOOKS**

Compass Books focuses on practical and informative 'how-to' books for writers. Written by experienced authors who also have extensive experience of tutoring at the most popular creative writing workshops, the books offer an insight into the more specialised niches of the publishing game.